The
Intelligence
Equation

This edition first published in 2009 by New Holland Publishers (UK) Ltd
London • Cape Town • Sydney • Auckland
www.newhollandpublishers.com

Garfield House, 86–88 Edgware Road, London W2 2EA, United Kingdom

10 9 8 7 6 5 4 3 2 1

Conceived and produced by
Elwin Street Productions
144 Liverpool Road
London N1 1LA
www.elwinstreet.com

ISBN 978 1 84773 501 0

Layouts designed by Louise Leffler

Picture credits: Corbis: 110; Dreamstime: pp. 25, 26, 37, 41, 42, 44, 47, 50, 54,
77, 87, 92, 96, 98, 104, 118, 127; iStock Photo: pp. 3, 9, 11, 13, 15, 19, 21, 22,
28, 30, 34, 49, 52, 59. 62. 64. 67 .69 .71 .73. 75. 76. 81, 83, 89, 91, 93, 95, 101,
102, 107, 112, 131, 116, 123, 135.

Printed in Singapore

Note: The author and publishers have made every effort to ensure that the
information given in this book is safe and accurate, but they cannot accept
liability for any resulting injury or loss or damage to either property or person,
whether direct or consequential and howsoever arising.

The
Intelligence
Equation

Stephen Pincock

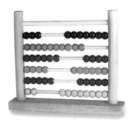

NEW
HOLLAND

Contents

Introduction

Have you ever fallen into bed at night, puzzling over an intractable problem, only to leap up the next morning, sharp as a razor, and find the answer was simple all along? If this sounds familiar, then you'll know that your intelligence is not a fixed thing. Mental sharpness can vary dramatically from time to time and situation to situation, depending on a whole host of factors – from the amount of sleep you've had to the kind of breakfast you ate.

Understanding the factors that help us to do a better job of reasoning, solving problems and learning from experience can make a big difference to our lives. Intelligence can help us do well at school, university and work, help us earn more and give us a chance to live more rewarding lives. But what is intelligence, exactly? Most experts will tell you that 'intelligence' is a complicated set of skills and abilities. In 1994, for example, 52 intelligence researchers signed a document that offered this definition:

Intelligence, they said, is, 'a very general mental capability that, among other things, involves the ability to reason, plan, solve problems, think abstractly, comprehend complex ideas, learn quickly and learn from experience. It is not merely book learning, a narrow academic skill, or test-taking smarts. Rather, it reflects a broader and deeper capability for comprehending our surroundings – catching on, making sense of things, or figuring out what to do.'

Over the years, people have developed various tests to try and boil down the different aspects of intelligence into simple scores – sometimes called IQ scores – which are used to compare people. The term 'IQ' was coined by a German psychologist called William Stern in 1912 as a way of scoring children's results on intelligence tests. These days, researchers use several different intelligence tests to generate scores that seek to measure a combination of knowledge, problem-solving and other abilities.

Interestingly, the various different tests of mental ability tend to rank individuals in roughly the same way. This has led many experts to believe that all our different thinking (or 'cognitive') abilities are reflections of a more fundamental, underlying general intelligence factor they call *g*. Some scientists break *g* down into two parts:

fluid intelligence, which is the ability to reason and solve new problems without using any knowledge you have previously acquired; and crystallised intelligence, the ability to use skills and knowledge you have previously gained.

So far, no one has developed a way to measure *g* exactly. At best, the different IQ tests that are used to measure intelligence can be said to estimate a person's general intelligence.

Nor do these tests take into consideration the fact that our mental abilities might vary from time to time and place to place. After all, nobody feels smart all of the time. Similarly, different people have different mental strengths. Creativity, memory, social intelligence, emotional intelligence and analytical skills have all been gathered under the umbrella of 'intelligence'. In the real world, each of these forms of intelligence matters a great deal.

It's a fact of life that many of the factors affecting our intelligence are beyond our control. Researchers who have studied the inheritance of intelligence, for example, have found that somewhere in the region of half the differences between people in IQ scores come down to their genetic inheritance from their parents. The circumstances of our early lives, which again are mostly out of our own control, are also vitally important. Good nutrition during infancy, a caring environment and access to education also make an enormous difference. At the other end of life, the ravages of time can wreak havoc on our cognitive abilities.

But this book is primarily about the factors we can influence. Despite the importance of genetics, upbringing and ageing, there are still plenty of things you can do to make the most of your intellectual inheritance, from lifestyle changes such as quitting smoking to specific brain-stimulating activities. This book is a guide to the fundamentals of intelligence in all its forms. Reading it will not necessarily alter your IQ, but it will show you ways to make the best of what you have, boost your performance and stay sharp.

Stephen Pincock

How to use this book

This book presents the 100 factors that most influence your mental sharpness and intelligence at any time, either positively or negatively. The information here is based on the latest medical and scientific research into the lifestyle factors, choices and activities that can affect your IQ, cognitive function and brainpower in general.

For each of the factors in the book, plus or minus points have been allocated to give you a sense of their relative impact on your overall intelligence and mental sharpness. If the science behind the information is particularly controversial or uncertain, a '?' motif has been added.

It is important to note that adding up your total score from the points assigned to these factors will not give you an IQ score or anything remotely like it. The points allocated to each factor are based on the relative importance of each one's impact on your general intelligence. So rather than adding up to a measure of your intelligence, the score will give you a sense of how well you are doing at making the most of your intelligence potential. So you can see if you are getting the most out of your brainpower consider the following scale:

Score
20 or over: You're really maximising your mental abilities
10–20:   You're doing well, but there's probably room for improvement
Under 10:   You could make more of your potential; look for ways to cut
                down on the negative factors in your life

Some of the factors in the book will affect your concentration or memory in the short term, others have an impact on your IQ and yet others will help determine how much of your cognitive function stays with you as you age. Strictly speaking these are all subtly different aspects of our mental functioning, but for you and me, it boils down to the same thing: staying in peak mental condition as you go through life.

In Part One, we look at factors that help get you off to a good start in life. Many of them have been shown to directly correlate with IQ. In Part Two, we move on to the lifestyle factors that can have an impact on your mental powers before looking at specific activities that can help you get smart in Part Three. If you want to boost your intelligence levels, try some of the positive activities, and make a concerted effort to avoid the negative ones.

Of course, all of these factors relate back eventually to the brain, so Part Four examines new evidence about the relationship between brain functions and intelligence, and looks at some of the ways we might be able to enhance our brain function in the future.

As you're adding up your points, remember to think of them as food for thought. If you find yourself accumulating minuses, don't be disheartened – it's never too late to change or do something to help yourself get smart.

Each of us is unique. Some of us love tomatoes; others prefer shellfish. She's a redhead; he's blond. Perhaps you enjoy blockbuster movies, or maybe you prefer the books of Virginia Woolf. We each walk, sing, jump and run in weird and wonderful ways.

Some of these characteristics we choose, while others appear to have been there since birth. So it is with our intelligence. Each of us differs in our capacity to plan, solve problems, understand complex ideas, adapt to our environment, learn from experience and so on. Some of these differences come about through our own choices, while others may have their origins in the fundamental facts of our lives.

In this chapter, we look at some of these basic facts of life. Some studies are controversial, such as the question of whether class or wealth can affect intelligence; others garner more universal agreement, such as the importance of good nutrition during infancy. What is important to remember is that the situation each of us is born into does not have to be a life sentence. Our circumstances are an important part of the story of human intelligence, but they are only a part of the story.

PART ONE

Life circumstances

1

Breastfeeding

+ 2 POINTS

Occasionally we use the word 'superfood' to describe something that is particularly nutritious or beneficial to us, for example, broccoli, blueberries or some types of algae. Whether or not this term has any significant meaning, there is one food that definitely meets that definition and that is breast milk. For the development of the body and intelligence, there's nothing better.

The World Health Organization (WHO) recommends that, ideally, babies should be given no other food or drink – not even water – before they reach six months of age. That is because breast milk protects the baby from infectious diseases such as diarrhoea and pneumonia, and promotes speedier recovery from any illness. Breastfeeding helps reduce the risk of ovarian cancer and breast cancer in mothers. All these benefits – and it's free.

When it comes to intelligence, scientific studies have charted a strong correlation between the intelligence of children and whether or not they were breastfed. In 2008 a study conducted in maternity hospitals in the Republic of Belarus concluded that children whose mothers had been actively encouraged to breastfeed did better in an intelligence test at age six. The study of almost 14,000 infants showed that breastfed children achieved higher scores in the parts of the test designed to test vocabulary, similarities and verbal IQ.

That study added strength to evidence that had already been accumulating and yet some scientists still question whether the apparent benefits of breast-feeding are actually due to differences in family background or upbringing. Danish researchers, in a study published in 2002, followed 3,000 people until they were in their 20s and 30s, looking at whether breastfeeding had had an impact on their adult intelligence. Crucially, the socio-economic and demographic status of all the families was noted at the beginning of the trial, allowing the researchers to take that into consideration in their results. They concluded that adults who had been breastfed as children had IQ scores roughly 6.6 points higher than their counterparts who had not been breastfed.

Exactly how breastfeeding might boost intelligence is not yet clear. It could be that the nutritional goodness in breast milk, including its blend of fatty acids, fosters the development of the brain. It might equally be that the physical and emotional act of breastfeeding accelerates brain development.

Either way, brainy kids do breast.

Recommendations on breastfeeding

WHO and UNICEF recommend:

- Initiation of breastfeeding within the first hour of life.

- Breastfeeding on demand – as often as the child desires, day and night.

- No use of bottles, teats or dummies.

- Exclusive breastfeeding – the infant receives only breast milk with no additional food or drink, not even water, up to the age of six months.

2

Childhood mistreatment

— 2 POINTS

Neglect and abuse can have devastating emotional and social effects on children, which may last a lifetime. Being the victim of mistreatment in childhood can also harm cognitive function and how well a child performs at school. Compared to non-maltreated children, those who suffer abuse and/or neglect have been shown to score significantly lower in a range of different measurements of intelligence.

It seems that neglect, particularly if it takes place early in life, can lead to problems that are particularly severe. In one study of 324 neglected children from New York State in the USA and a matched group of children who were not neglected, the neglected children performed less well at school, had lower grades and were more likely to have to repeat school years.

According to a review published in 2002 by Canadian researchers, neglected children have more severe cognitive and academic deficiencies than those who are physically abused. There is also evidence that maltreatment results in physical and chemical harm to the brain. Researchers have found signs of changes in brain functioning that relate to the body's response to stress. Other evidence suggests that maltreated children have smaller brain volumes, and suffer a range of different structural and chemical changes.

3

Early crawling
0.5 POINTS ✚

Learning to move around under their own steam is one of the most significant stages in the lives of young children. Suddenly there are places to explore, people to meet, lessons to be learned. Given the difference that moving around makes to an infant's experience of the world, it is perhaps not surprising that researchers have found it also enhances cognitive development. As researcher Joseph Campos from the University of California-Berkeley puts it 'travel broadens the mind'.

In one experiment, for example, researchers showed that infants who were crawling by nine months of age and infants who were walking by 12 months of age had a greater understanding of language and of the permanence of things than infants who were not crawling or walking at the same ages.

It also seems that children who achieve their milestones earlier have different cognitive function later in life. In one study, infants in Finland who could stand early scored higher on certain cognitive tests (but not on others) when in their 30s. Another research group from Australia reported that infants who had better motor skills, such as crawling, walking and sitting up, in the first two years of life had better cognitive performance when they began school.

All of this comes with some caveats, however. At this stage, it is not clear whether learning motor skills actually leads to changes in the way the brain works or whether it is simply a developmental stage that comes before those changes.

4

Maternal drug use

— 3 POINTS

Every year, millions of pregnant women around the world use drugs such as tobacco, alcohol and narcotics. Doing so exposes their unborn child to a high risk of poor health once they are born, including low birth weight and other complications that can blight their intellectual achievement.

In terms of legal drugs, both alcohol and tobacco are known to have harmful effects on babies while in the womb. Although most women who drink small amounts of alcohol during pregnancy do not harm the long-term health of their babies, heavy or long-term abuse can interfere with a child's future health, including their intellectual development. That is why many professional groups now advise women to steer clear of alcohol during pregnancy.

Moving on to illicit drugs, children born to mothers who use opiate drugs, such as heroin, can experience neonatal withdrawal syndrome, which typically includes wakefulness, jitteriness and other symptoms of cerebral irritability. This can play havoc with the growing bond between mother and infant, affecting the baby's long-term emotional and cognitive development.

The list goes on: cocaine exposure in the womb can result in poor mental development and long-lasting impairment of the brain; benzodiazepines can cause neurological and behavioural impairments and neonatal withdrawal symptoms. Mothers who use amphetamines may give birth to babies who are irritable and agitated or who suffer drowsiness that may result in poor feeding. The bottom line: avoid drugs if you want to give your child the best chance of a bright future.

5

Having a younger father
2 POINTS

Children born to younger dads have a better chance of doing well on tests of thinking skills, researchers found in 2009. Their study looked at data on more than 33,000 full-term children born to mothers in the USA from 1959 to 1965, who had been tested for their ability to think and reason at the ages of eight months, four years and seven years. They found that concentration, learning, speaking, reading, arithmetic and memory were worse for the children of older fathers.

As if that isn't worrying enough, intelligence isn't the only factor hit by a father's age. Other researchers have also shown that the children of older dads are at greater risk of health problems such as birth defects, autism and schizophrenia. Consider the current trend for men to wait until they are older to have children and you can see that there might be a problem looming.

One theory currently being explored is that DNA in the sperm of older men might contain more DNA errors. But researchers also think other factors are at play. When they took into account socio-economic factors, for example, they found that the impact of a father's age was somewhat reduced. For example, the average score on the Stanford Binet Intelligence Scale test was nearly six points lower for children born to fathers age 50 compared to those born to fathers age 20. But when the socio-economic factors were taken into account, the difference dropped to 2.2 points.

The study does not mean that all children of older men will have lower IQs, but it does suggest that something is going on to increase the risk of subtle reductions in cognitive ability in those children. On the other hand, children in the study with older mothers tended to perform better on tests of cognitive ability. That finding, which chimes with other studies, suggests that the generally higher income and education levels of older mothers are associated with more nurturing home environments.

Infant nutrition

✚ 5 POINTS

Around the world, millions of children die before their fifth birthday – 10 million in 2006 alone. The biggest cause? The simple fact that they have not had enough nutritious food.

Those who do manage to survive prolonged malnutrition are likely to suffer long-term consequences. According to a paper in *The Lancet*, a medical journal, malnutrition in the first two years of life is irreversible. Malnourished children grow up with poor health, and their own children tend to be small. In the view of the World Health Organization, hunger is the gravest single threat to global public health.

Prolonged malnutrition during childhood also has lingering effects on intellectual performance in later life. In one study, pre-schoolers in two Guatemalan villages (where undernourishment is a common occurrence) were given access to as much protein supplement as they needed over the course of several years. A decade later, many of them scored significantly higher on

---

How to boost mental sharpness through nutrition

The World Health Organization's five key measures provide the basis for a brain-food diet:

- Feed your baby only breast milk for the first six months of life.

- Eat a variety of foods.

- Eat plenty of vegetables and fruits.

- Eat moderate amounts of fat and oils.

- Eat less salt and sugars.

school tests than children in similar villages and circumstances who had not been given supplements. Even in cases where malnutrition is not involved, dietary supplements can influence intelligence. Some studies have shown that children who were not suffering from malnutrition and received vitamin and mineral supplements achieved better test scores than those in control groups who were given inactive placebos.

Exactly how nutrition affects intellect is not easy to describe with certainty. Some of the effects may not be direct, as malnourished children tend to be less responsive to adults and less motivated to learn than their counterparts who receive enough to eat. Also, malnourished children often come from families who are disadvantaged in a number of ways, dealing with issues such as poverty, overcrowding and unclean water.

Nevertheless, tackling malnutrition need not be complicated: breastfeeding advice, dietary supplements and improvements in hygiene have all been shown to help. Given all this, it is clear that tackling infant malnutrition is an essential task.

7

Low birth weight
— 2 POINTS

'It's a girl! She's seven pounds!' Ask any new parent how much their baby weighed at birth and most will be able to tell you in a heartbeat. Along with the gender, it is one of the first facts parents learn about their offspring. Could it be that this simple measurement will have an influence on the baby's future intelligence?

Birth weight is a key predictor of a child's later development. Babies who are born with low birth weights have consistently been shown to be at increased risk of diabetes, obesity and other problems as they grow up. On the other hand, girls with high birth weight might be more likely to develop rheumatic diseases.

Birth weight also has an effect on intelligence. Children born at low birth weight, which is defined as below 2,500 g (5 lbs 8 oz), have deficiencies in average intelligence test scores once they reach school. Among those who are classified as being low birth weight, children who are smaller at birth have more problems than those closer to normal birth weight.

More recently, researchers have begun to look at whether the link between birth weight and intelligence extends into the normal weight range and have found that it does. Scientists in the USA studied data taken from 3,484 children born between 1959 and 1966 with birth weights that ranged from 1,500 g (3 lbs 5 oz) to 3,999 g (8 lbs 13 oz). Comparing the children's IQ at age seven, they found that among boys, but not girls, every 100 g (4 oz) change in birth weight correlated to an increase in IQ of 0.5 per cent.

Now this difference is not enough to be significant between individual children, but it could be when we think of whole populations. If scientists can get a better handle on the factors that affect birth weight among normal birth weight babies, it could have a significant impact on average intelligence levels in the overall population.

Being tall

1 POINT

On average, tall people tend to have higher IQ scores than short people. Scientists have calculated that overall about four per cent of the variation in IQ within a population is explained by variations in height. Of course, nobody sensible suggests for a moment that there are no highly intelligent short people (or less sharp beanpoles) but the correlation is still fascinating. Why should it be so?

The most likely explanation seems to be that height and intelligence result from the same influences. For example, in some cases being tall is a sign that a person was well-nourished as a baby; this is also known to influence intelligence. There are also likely to be genetic factors at play, influencing both height and intelligence. Studies of twins in the Netherlands and Norway have certainly suggested that this might be the case.

In the 1980s, US researchers compared IQ scores and height in a group of 2,000 children that they studied over a period of five years, first when they were eight, and again at 13. While they found a correlation between the two characteristics at both ages, there was no association between growing taller and gains in IQ. The results suggest that the link between height and IQ must happen early in childhood, at least before the age of eight.

Other researchers suggest that the association begins much earlier than that. One study shows that the length of infants aged between five and 12 months correlates with measures of speed at which information is processed.

High-quality pre-school

✚ 2 POINTS

Researchers from North Carolina, USA showed in the 1970s that early childhood education can have positive effects on the cognitive development of children.

Their study, called the Carolina Abecedarian Project, involved more than 100 children from very disadvantaged backgrounds. Half of them were given full-time, high-quality education from infancy until the age of five, and the remainder received no particular treatment, although they often did use child care and pre-school resources available in the community.

The Abecedarian education (which takes its name from the word once used to describe the youngest students in 19th-century American schools, who were named A-B-C-Darians or abecedarians because they were just learning their alphabet, or 'a-b-cs') was provided all day, five days per week, year-round. Children received close attention from teachers and were given a systematic curriculum of 'educational games' that helped with social, emotional and cognitive development, with a particular focus on language.

By the time the children had reached the age of 21, there were noticeable differences in their lives. Compared to the children who did not undergo the special pre-school programme, the Abecedarian-educated children had better results in reading and mathematics tests. They also showed modestly better IQ scores, gaining an extra 4.4 points on average in a full-scale IQ test, and 4.2 points better in verbal IQ. And the children who participated in the programme also completed more years of education and were more likely to attend university.

In another study, the Perry Pre-school Project, researchers followed 128 children, 64 of whom were provided with high-quality pre-school education every weekday morning for up to two years between the ages of three and four. The curriculum emphasised active learning, including decision-making and problem-solving. At the age of 27, the pre-school educated children had completed an average of almost one full year more of schooling and were significantly more likely to have graduated from university.

How to encourage your pre-schooler to learn

- Keep reading. Nurture a love for books with trips to the library or bookshop.

- Encourage your child to play with other children, a great way to learn the value of sharing and friendship.

- Help your child's vocabulary by speaking to him or her in complete sentences and in 'adult' language.

- Encourage him or her to use correct words and phrases.

- Help your pre-schooler learn numerals and simple arithmetic with games that use household items. Make it fun.

High testosterone levels

+ **0.5 POINTS**

Mention testosterone to most people and they may think of hairy chests, powerful muscles and sexual potency. While all of these characteristics are definitely associated with testosterone levels, this vital hormone plays a much broader part in the lives of men, and women, including a role in the way our brain functions.

Boys and girls who are exposed to high levels of testosterone in the womb, for example, are more likely to develop traits typical of autism, including a preference for solitary activities and strong skills in working with numbers and recognising patterns. Cambridge researcher Simon Baron-Cohen has suggested that human brains are largely attuned either to empathising with others or to understanding how systems work. Women are more likely to be in the first group and men in the second, he suggests, while autistic people have extreme versions of a brain type that is common among men in the population at large.

There is growing evidence too that testosterone is important in the decline in brain function that takes place as we age. Researchers have known for some time that testosterone levels drop as we age, just as many of us start to notice problems with our memory. More recently they have begun to report that the first phenomenon might be responsible for the second.

In one study of 407 men over the age of 50, researchers from the US National Institutes of Health found that those whose testosterone levels remained high did best on tests of memory. Other studies have linked higher testosterone levels in mid-life with better preservation of tissue in some parts of the brain.

So does this mean that men should take testosterone supplements to help them hang on to their mental faculties? So far, the jury is out. A few short-term studies have provided some positive evidence, but researchers warn that this needs to be balanced with the potential risks of taking the supplements.

Higher socio-economic class
0.5 POINTS +

There is a direct correlation between socio-economic status, as measured by family income, parental education level and occupation, and scores in intelligence tests. Numerous studies over the years have found that on average, the higher a person's socio-economic status, the higher their IQ scores and level of academic achievement. Of course, the key word in that sentence is 'average'. Nobody is saying for a minute there are no geniuses among lower-income families – or no dimwits among the rich.

Researchers have suggested that the relationship may work in two ways. Firstly, there is the role of genetics, which might mean that higher or lower IQs are hereditary to some extent. Then it also seems that the environment you grow up in can have an impact on your developing intelligence. For example, there is evidence that IQ scores can predict how well you will do at school, and that education is a major determinant of occupational class.

On the other hand, it looks as though intelligence can also affect a person's ability to alter their socio-economic status: researchers have shown that scores on intelligence tests seem to predict a person's likelihood of moving out of the social class of their parents to a higher or lower one.

So while there is a correlation between class and intelligence, in no way is a person's intelligence wholly dependent on their socio-economic situation.

12

Poverty

— 2 POINTS

Growing up in a family where there is insufficient money to properly meet basic needs for food, clothing and shelter can have a significantly harmful effect on a child's intellect.

Children in families whose total income was less than half the official poverty threshold scored between six and 13 points lower in tests of IQ, verbal ability and achievement. That is a large difference from an educational point of view. As the authors of that study point out, a six- to 13-point difference in IQ might mean the difference between being placed in a special education class or not.

Other researchers have shown that the harm that poverty causes can be strong enough to outweigh the effects of genetic inheritance. One study, using an IQ test known as the Wechsler Intelligence Scale for Children, showed that in twins raised near or below the poverty level, 60 per cent of differences in IQ between individuals was accounted for by their shared environment; in affluent families, the result was almost exactly the reverse.

Understanding how poverty has this impact is not simple, but researchers have shown that differences in the home environment, such as the availability of reading materials and toys, and parental discipline and parent-child interaction, make a big difference.

HIV

3 POINTS —

In 2007, the United Nations estimated that roughly 33 million people around the globe were infected with HIV. Declines in mental processes are common among people living with the virus, particularly the many millions who do not yet have access to anti-HIV drugs.

The specific symptoms of HIV-associated dementia (also called AIDS dementia complex) vary from person to person, but they can include diminishing reasoning, judgment, concentration and problem-solving as well as failing memory. Other symptoms include changes in personality and behaviour, speech problems and clumsiness. These symptoms are a consequence of the virus infecting white blood cells that travel into the brain and spinal cord.

The development of anti-HIV drug combinations that are able to control virus levels in the body has seen the frequency of AIDS dementia complex decline in Western countries. Without the drugs, roughly half the people infected with HIV develop symptoms of dementia. With them, the incidence drops to less than 20 per cent.

Thankfully, treatment with effective combinations of anti-AIDS drugs does not only prevent or delay the onset of AIDS dementia complex; it can also improve mental function in those who already have it.

14

Kidney disease
— 1 POINT

People with diabetes, high blood pressure and other such health problems can be at risk of chronic renal disease, a condition that leads to the gradual destruction of the kidneys. The results of several studies have now shown that medical problems associated with the kidneys can also have a negative impact on your mental faculties.

US researchers who looked at a large, ethnically diverse group of people aged between 20 and 60 found that those who had moderate kidney disease were more likely to suffer poorer visual attention and worse learning and concentration than others.

Another study found that there was a direct correlation between worsening kidney disease and slower brain responses. The researchers who did that study concluded that increasingly severe kidney disease is associated with progressive cognitive decline.

Although cognitive decline has been noted as a common occurrence in patients with chronic kidney disease, it is unclear if this is due to the patients' advanced age, their health conditions or the treatments they receive.The good news for people with kidney disease who are able to have kidney transplants, however, is that a transplantation can improve their mental performance. In 2008, US researchers assessed cognitive performance before and after kidney transplantation in 37 patients and compared the results to 13 patients who did not receive kidney transplants but received dialysis. The results showed a statistically significant improvement in performance on tests of verbal learning and memory, attention and language after patients received kidney transplants. So you should be looking after your kidneys and doing what you can to keep them healthy, not just for your overall physical health, but for your cognitive functions as well.

How to keep your kidneys healthy

- Eat plenty of fruit and vegetables including peas, beans and grain-based food.

- Eat lean meat like chicken and fish each week.

- Limit your intake of salty or fatty food.

- Drink plenty of water, which lessens the risk of kidney stones forming.

- Stay fit and maintain a healthy weight. Adults should exercise at a moderate pace for 30 minutes or more on most days.

- Don't smoke. Cigarette-smoking slows the flow of blood to the kidneys and increases the risk of kidney cancer.

- Limit your alcohol intake to two small drinks per day if you are male or one small drink per day if you are female.

- Have your blood pressure checked regularly, and discuss with your doctor any other appropriate medical tests, such as regular blood or urine tests.

15

Chemotherapy
1 POINT

'Chemobrain' is a phrase cancer patients use to describe the mental fog that can accompany treatment for cancer. Sufferers find they can't focus, remember or multitask the way they could before the treatment.

For years, some clinicians doubted whether the phenomenon was anything more than a figment of their patients' imagination, but more recent research has given support to the claim that it is real. A study from the University of California, Los Angeles showed that chemotherapy causes changes to the brain's metabolism and blood flow that can persist for at least 10 years after treatment.

Researchers used positron emission tomography (PET) to scan the brains of 21 women who had undergone surgery to remove breast tumours between five and 10 years earlier. Sixteen of them had been treated with chemotherapy to reduce the risk of cancer recurrence. As the women performed a series of short-term memory exercises, the researchers measured blood flow to their brains and also ran a scan of resting brain metabolism after they finished the exercises.

The scans revealed that blood flow to the frontal cortex and cerebellum spiked as the chemotherapy patients performed the memory tests, indicating a rapid jump in these brain regions' activity level. In essence, these women's brains were having to work harder than normal to recall the information.

Exactly what causes chemobrain remains a mystery. Experts suggest it could be caused by a number of factors such as the cancer itself, chemotherapy drugs, other drugs used as part of treatment (such as anti-nausea or pain medicines) or stress. According to conservative estimates, 20 to 30 per cent of people who have chemotherapy will experience chemobrain.

16

Thyroid disease
1 POINT ▬

The thyroid gland, located in your neck just below your Adam's apple, produces hormones that regulate how quickly your body uses energy and makes proteins, and sensitivity to other hormones.

Doctors have known for many years that diseases that make the thyroid overactive or underactive can cause dementia. More recently, some researchers have found that even subtle changes in thyroid hormones can affect our thinking.

In one study, researchers followed almost 2,000 older men and women for 12 years, looking at the link between thyroid hormone levels and the risk of Alzheimer's disease. They found that women whose levels of thyroid-stimulating hormones were either high or low had an increased risk of going on to develop Alzheimer's disease.

Chinese researchers, meanwhile, found that women whose thyroid activity was slightly lower than normal had impairments in their working memory – the memory you use for temporarily storing and using information. Interestingly, the researchers gave the women synthetic forms of thyroid hormone for six months and then tested them again. Their results showed that with the addition of the synthetic hormone, their memory performance had improved.

Mental health problems

+ # 1 POINT

The Greek philosopher Aristotle said that there is no great genius without some touch of madness. In all the centuries since he gave voice to this seemingly paradoxical idea – that great intelligence often goes hand in hand with mental illness – it has lost none of its currency.

In the 1970s, a study of 42 English and French poets found evidence of significant psychiatric illness in 45 per cent of them; 20 years later, another researcher surveyed 1,004 20th-century artists and writers and found that 74 per cent of them had shown signs of mental illness.

If anything, the link seems to have gained greater credence these days than ever before – if the Internet is anything to go by. Lists of geniuses who suffered conditions such as manic depression (now known as bipolar disorder) or schizophrenia abound, including author Charles Dickens, musician Thelonius Monk and the mathematical prodigy John Nash.

But how might madness promote genius? There are a few possibilities. The manic phase of bipolar disorder, for example, is associated with quick thinking, greater verbal fluency and self-confidence, while schizophrenic people can experience sudden jumps in their thought processes, known as Knight's Move thinking, which can free them from following preconceived patterns.

Among people with autism, there are also many examples of individuals who have remarkable gifts in the fields of music, mathematics and art. Around one in 10 people with autism are said to have these kinds of 'savant' abilities and modern techniques in brain-imaging genetic analysis are beginning to reveal some of the ways they emerge. For Hans Asperger, an early pioneer in the study of autism, the link harked back to Aristotle. 'For success in science and art,' Asperger wrote, 'a dash of autism is essential.'

18

Ageing

4 POINTS —

As we get older, many of us notice parts of our bodies showing distinct signs of wear and tear – knees start creaking, backs begin to ache, hair turns grey, eyesight fades. Our brains are not immune to degeneration either.

Specific age-related changes that start from around age 60 are associated with fading memory and mental agility. Dementia is a word used to describe the progressive decline in our mental faculties beyond what might be expected from normal ageing. Sufferers can experience memory loss combined with other signs of cognitive decline, including difficulty with language and with carrying out specific physical actions. The most common form of dementia is Alzheimer's disease, which accounts for more than half of dementia cases.

The proportion of people with dementia is thought to double every five years from the age of 65. Some scientists have estimated that 5 per cent of people aged 65 have dementia, a figure that rises as high as 50 per cent for those aged 85–90. There is no question that it is a terrible experience to endure, but there are actions we can take to help ward off or slow the effects of ageing on the brain.

How to ward off dementia

- Reduce your risk of vascular dementia by quitting tobacco, lowering your blood pressure and taking exercise.

- Keep your mind active – learn new tasks, socialise, play board games or puzzles.

- Limit your intake of alcoholic drinks to one or two per day.

- Avoid head injuries. (Experts believe head injuries may increase the risk of developing Alzheimer's disease.)

Living in modern times
+ 5 POINTS

Over recent decades, scientists have noticed a remarkable thing about intelligence: IQ scores are on the rise. Since the first tests were introduced in the early twentieth century, each new generation seems to do better than their predecessors. The average rise seems to be around three IQ points per decade.

This phenomenon, known as the Flynn effect in honour of the researcher James R. Flynn who did much to document its occurrence, leaves researchers baffled. Does it mean that humanity is getting more intelligent or just that we are getting better at IQ tests? Is each generation noticeably smarter than those who came before? James Flynn himself points out that this is not really the right way to think about the question. Instead, he stresses the importance of dissecting 'intelligence' into different skills, such as solving mathematical problems, interpreting works of literature and finding rapid solutions. 'The twentieth century saw some cognitive skills make great gains, while others were in the doldrums,' he writes.

Flynn and others also point out that the modern cultural environment is much more intellectually stimulating than that of our ancestors. Each successive generation has been exposed to far richer communications, such as television and computers, than the one before. In short, he says that environmental changes arising from modernisation have meant that people are now far more used to manipulating abstract concepts than they were a century ago.

It might also be that other factors have played a part: nutrition, a trend towards smaller families and better education might have contributed to the rise in IQ scores. Whatever the causes, the most recent research shows that in some parts of the world at least, the rises are continuing.

20

Genetic inheritance
2 POINTS —

If one of your parents has been diagnosed with Alzheimer's disease or dementia, then the chances are you're more likely to develop memory problems yourself in middle age, scientists have found. Genetics plays a role in passing dementia risk between generations, experts say.

US researchers made this finding when studying three generations of people in a large project known as the Framingham Heart study. The first generation has been followed since 1948. The researchers studied 715 people whose average age was 59. Of this group, 282 of them had one or both parents with dementia. Everyone was tested for a gene known to be a risk factor for dementia, known as ApoE-e4.

From this study, researchers found that there was a difference in memory between the two groups, which was equivalent to about 15 years of brain ageing. That effect was largely limited to those participants who had the ApoE-e4 gene.

Although the findings are important, they do not suggest that everyone with the gene will develop Alzheimer's. The best research so far suggests that the gene plays a role in about half of Alzheimer's cases. As yet, the study has not gone on to show how many of the people with memory deficits in middle age will go on to develop dementia.

For now, perhaps the best way to deal with this information is to use it in a positive way. If one of your parents has dementia, then there's more incentive to do all you can to boost your cognitive functions.

In Part One we pondered some of the circumstances of life that have an impact on your brainpower. Like the genes we inherit from our parents, many of those factors are beyond our ability to change. (Although parents might want to think about whether they can change them in their children's lives.)

In the following pages, the opposite is true. Here we begin exploring the effects of the lifestyle choices we make every day: choices we have control over and can change. The way you live your life, what you eat and drink, how much sleep you get and your overall mood all alter your mental sharpness, so if you want to make the most of your intellect you need to pay attention to all these elements.

What's more, making a change in your life can help you maintain your mental agility and memory as you age. In general, our memory and thinking speed declines as we grow older – a process that can lead to dementia. But science shows us that there are ways to help ward off these changes. By the choices we make during our lives, we can avoid damaging our brains, repair some of the harm that has been done and forge new neural connections. It's never too late to make a difference.

PART TWO

Lifestyle

A good night's sleep

+ 2 POINTS

In his great play *Macbeth*, William Shakespeare described sleep as the 'balm of hurt minds… chief nourisher in life's feast'. In terms of intelligence, it seems he was right. It is becoming clear that sleep plays an important role in our ability to learn and remember, particularly for the types of memory that help us to learn skills.

In 2008, US researchers showed that sleep helps the mind learn complicated tasks and helps people recover learning they otherwise thought they had lost over the course of a day. In the previous year, another group showed that the ability to make logical 'big picture' inferences from disparate pieces of information depended on taking a break from studies and getting a good night's sleep.

Their results suggest that sleep doesn't just strengthen memories, it helps you knit them together and understand how they are related to one another. Some researchers have suggested this could even be the primary purpose of sleep: during the day, you gather pieces of the puzzle and while you sleep your mind puts them together.

How to get a good night's sleep

- Maintain a regular sleep schedule.

- Establish a bedtime ritual, such as taking a bath or reading, that can help sleep to come more easily.

- Control your room environment and temperature, as being too cold or too hot can disrupt sleep.

- Take exercise. Exercising during the day can help you to sleep well at night.

- Avoid caffeine. Caffeine is a stimulant and notorious for keeping people awake.

- Avoid alcohol. It too can prevent proper deep sleep.

Sleep apnea
3 POINTS —

A good night's sleep can do wonders for your ability to think clearly, but what happens when sleep is chronically disrupted by conditions such as sleep apnea?

Sleep apnea is a breathing disorder that affects approximately 2 per cent of children and 5 per cent of adults. Sufferers repeatedly stop breathing for short periods during the night, causing the levels of oxygen in their blood to temporarily drop. People who experience such disturbances on a regular basis, particularly during childhood, can suffer lasting damage to their cognitive powers.

Doctors have known for some time that people with sleep apnea can have trouble thinking clearly, remembering and concentrating. But more recently, worrying new results have shown that children with untreated sleep apnea can suffer permanent harm to brain structures that are tied to learning ability.

Scientists from Johns Hopkins University in the USA compared 19 children with severe obstructive sleep apnea with 12 children without the disorder. Children with the condition had lower average IQ test scores, did worse on tests of memory and word fluency, and showed evidence of structural changes to parts of the brain vital to learning, memory and higher-level thinking.

'This should be a wake-up call to both parents and doctors that undiagnosed or untreated sleep apnea might hurt children's brains,' researcher Dr Ann Halbower said after her results were published.

In children, the leading cause of sleep apnea is enlarged tonsils and adenoids, and the first choice for therapy is surgical removal. Another treatment – one that is commonly used in adults – involves wearing a special mask at night to ensure smooth airflow and uninterrupted breathing.

Antidepressant medication

+ **0.5 POINTS**

It is a sad reality that being depressed is a risk factor in declining mental sharpness and may be a factor in developing dementia. It was therefore particularly bad news that some antidepressants – a class of drugs known as tricyclic antidepressants – have side effects that include disorientation and memory impairment.

This might seem strange – that a depression treatment should have the same effect on cognition as depression itself. But the reason is that tricyclic antidepressants (and several other types of drugs) have the effect of blocking the brain-signalling chemical acetylcholine, which is required for memory.

For this reason, tricyclic antidepressants are not used as often in older patient groups. Instead, new classes of antidepressants are increasingly used and these appear to have fewer side effects. Examples include drugs known as selective serotonin reuptake inhibitors (SSRIs).

These new medications actually seem to improve cognitive function, rather than making it worse. In some studies, patients taking the drugs have experienced improved vigilance, attention and memory. In one example, researchers even found that an SSRI, called sertraline, improved mental sharpness in people who had suffered a traumatic brain injury.

Disappointingly, in most cases it seems that the improvement offered by these drugs does not bring cognitive function back up to normal. But one study has shown particularly good results with the drug bupropion – one of the top four most-prescribed antidepressants in the USA – finding that patients treated with it saw their cognitive performance rise to the level of non-depressed people. Plus, bupropion also helps people quit smoking, another benefit in the cognitive stakes.

View of trees
0.5 POINTS

One February day in 1913, American poet Alfred Joyce Kilmer was working in his home, overlooking a wooded hillside thick with oaks, maples and birches. The lines he wrote that day have become his most enduring legacy: 'I think that I shall never see, a poem as lovely as a tree.' In fact, had he but known it at the time, trees have more than just their appearance going for them. It transpires that gazing at nature has a remarkable capacity to restore concentration and improve self-discipline.

In one study, scientists compared 145 residents living in two public housing buildings in Chicago: one building was surrounded by concrete and asphalt, the other by pockets of leafy green. Residents in the greener setting showed better performance in a test designed to measure their ability to attend to a task.

In a second study of 169 inner-city children, which explored the relationship between the amount of natural surroundings they had near their homes and three different forms of self-discipline, the leafiness of the area accounted for 20 per cent of differences in their scores in girls; the link was not so strong for boys, although the researchers suggest this could be because boys tend to play further from home.

Why should this be so? Scientists say that the human brain has two levels of attention: directed attention, which we use to concentrate on work, and involuntary attention, which happens when we respond to things like wild animals or nature.

Directed attention is a finite resource. According to 'attention restoration theory', walks in nature help renew this resource by capturing our involuntary attention, and giving our directed attention a break.

Sunshine

+ # 1 POINT

Just getting out into the sunshine – or turning on brighter lights – is enough to help stimulate the parts of your brain needed for alertness, researchers have found. Bright light can also have a positive effect on the symptoms of dementia.

There may be a few reasons why light is good for the brain. In one study, UK scientists probed the workings of the brain using a technique called functional magnetic resonance imaging or fMRI. It shows brain activity by measuring blood flow to different parts of the brain when people are involved in different activities.

They tested the response of the brain to sounds before and after a person's eye was exposed to a bright white light. They found a remarkably direct effect: bright light very quickly raised activity levels in parts of the brain involved in alertness.

US researchers found more evidence of the way light can boost your thinking power in a study of older people in 12 different care facilities. In some of the homes, the researchers installed brighter lights for use all day long and in others they kept the lights dim. After up to three and a half years of this intervention, the people in the brighter homes had moderately less disturbed cognition, better mood and behaviour, and slept better at night.

The researchers think that the beneficial effect that light seems to have might act by helping the brain's pacemaker region (known as the suprachiasmatic nucleus) to synchronise rhythms in our hormones and metabolism, thereby improving overall functioning.

Another way sunlight can affect the brain is via vitamin D. This vitamin is found in only a few foods; most of our vitamin D comes from exposure to sunlight when ultraviolet light converts a chemical in the skin to vitamin D. There is very good evidence that vitamin D is important for the development and function of the brain – including the fact that there are receptors for the vitamin throughout the brain. Vitamin D also has the capacity to affect proteins in the brain that are directly involved in learning and memory.

US researchers recently found that older people who had low levels of vitamin D in their systems tended to do worse in tests that measured their mental faculties. They suggest that maintaining adequate vitamin D levels might be vital for retaining cognitive function.

How to safely increase your time spent in the sun

- Get outdoors regularly: to boost your brainpower take a stroll through a park, take the dog for a walk, play a game of tennis or take part in any other activity that will take you outside.

- Work near a window: it can be difficult to get out into the sun if you are confined to an office all day, but if possible, do your thinking near sources of sunlight.

- Try light therapy: in situations where there isn't much natural light, specially designed 'light therapy' lights can mimic natural light.

- Take sensible precautions when spending time in the sun; wear sunscreen and protective clothing to shield you from the harmful effects of the sun's rays, and drink plenty of water if you are out on a hot day.

26

Pregnancy

+ 0.5 POINTS

Does pregnancy turn your brain to mush? According to the popular myth it does. After all, many new mothers complain of memory lapses and other manifestations of 'baby brain'. But science does not support this. In fact, there is good evidence that the opposite may be the case, and that having a baby may boost your brainpower.

By studying mice, rats and humans, researchers have shown that the hormonal changes during pregnancy remodel the brain. Some studies have shown that becoming a mother stimulates parts of the brain known to govern maternal behaviour. Others have shown that it boosts neuron size in the brain region known as the hippocampus, which is involved in memory, learning and emotions. In studies of rats, mothers have been shown to navigate mazes more efficiently, have less anxiety and fear and excel at multiskilling.

In 2008, a team of Australian researchers showed that in human mothers, memory and brain functioning speed were no different from those of childless women. Their study gathered data from several tests conducted on a group of women in 1999 and again in 2007.

So why does the 'baby brain' myth persist? Researcher Helen Christensen suggests that in studies examining memory capacity, people sometimes think there is a problem when there is none, or they attribute normal 'dippiness' to pregnancy. It is also likely that a regular feature of new parenthood – chronic sleep deprivation – has an effect. In other words, if you are pregnant and feel as if you cannot think straight, don't worry too much. It's nothing a few years of sound sleep won't fix.

Stress

1 POINT   —

Here is some good advice from researchers who study intelligence: chill out, it might improve your cognitive function.

In various studies, stress has been linked to poorer performance in tests that measure attention and processing speed. In one study, children and adolescents who suffered from post-traumatic stress disorder were found to have lower IQ scores. In other work, researchers suggested that people who suffer long-term stress may find themselves struggling with strategic thinking and memory.

Scientists think the link may be a hormone called cortisol. Stress causes the body to release more cortisol, which can prevent the brain from laying down a new memory or accessing memories that already exist. In 2008, researchers showed that raising or lowering the amount of the hormone in young squirrels rendered the animals less able to learn how to respond to danger.

Thankfully, stress reduction techniques – together with wider lifestyle changes – have been shown to boost the efficiency of parts of the brain dedicated to working memory. So if you want your brain to perform at top speed, take the time to de-stress.

Tips for combating stress

- Identify your triggers. What are the sources of your stress? Can you change the patterns that lead to these situations?

- Daily meditation can help quiet the mind and induce deep relaxation.

- Modify your reactions. Experts say it is possible to train yourself to react to events in ways that make them less stressful.

- Have a massage. Research has shown that it is an effective tonic for stress.

Being sociable

3 POINTS

Intelligence is much more than being good at maths or languages. According to the psychologist Howard Gardner, there are nine types of intelligence, ranging from sensitivity to the natural world, to the capacity to think in three dimensions. One of the most significant types is social intelligence – the ability to understand and interact with others.

Psychologist Daniel Goleman argues that in modern society, outstanding leaders need a combination of self-mastery and social intelligence. He cites research showing that high social intelligence predicts how well banking executives do in their annual appraisals. Catholic priests with high social intelligence also apparently have more satisfied parishioners.

In 1999, US researchers studied nearly 3,000 elderly people and correlated their mental status with the number of social contacts they had. Those with no social contacts were approximately twice as likely to develop cognitive problems compared to those with five or six social contacts.

Researchers think social intelligence became increasingly significant as human societies became more complex. In fact, research shows that social intelligence in primate species is linked to increasing brain size. Some scientists argue that the ability to learn from others may have played a pivotal role in the evolution of the human brain.

But is social intelligence simply general intelligence applied in a social setting? The modern discipline of social neuroscience suggests not. Studies of the brain during social encounters show that our social behaviour is guided as much by instinct as by the kind of rational thought processes associated with mental effort.

The good news is that being sociable, like most human attributes, is a skill you can work on, so you can try and learn from others who do well in social situations.

Depression

2 POINTS —

Depression is an awful condition that affects virtually all aspects of a person's life and intellectual functioning is not spared. In fact, one of the defining characteristics of depression is a waning ability to concentrate or think clearly.

Perhaps more worryingly, it also seems that symptoms of depression can be associated with cognitive decline in elderly people. In other words, those who show signs of depression are at greater risk of developing dementia. It is not clear why this should be, but some scientists have suggested that chronic depression causes the release of specific hormones that can damage the hippocampus, a part of the brain that is important in memory and processing information about the physical world around us.

Interestingly, it is not only chronic depression that can have an impact on the sharpness of your thinking. A recent study showed that US college students suffering 'seasonal affective disorder' – a form of depression in which depressive episodes occur in the autumn or winter, and resolve in spring – also reported problems with perception, attention and retrieving memories.

Happily, there is some evidence that dealing with depression has a positive impact. In the 1990s, for example, one group of researchers looked at the IQ of patients with depression before and after treatment. They found that the depressed people had a 'pronounced deficit' when it came to parts of IQ tests that deal with problem solving, puzzles and reasoning. After treatment (with electroconvulsive therapy in this study) their IQ scores were improved.

Getting an education

+ **3 POINTS**

The relationship between education and intelligence is a two-way street. In both directions, it's positive.

Firstly, children with higher intelligence test scores tend to do better at school – they are less likely to drop out, are more likely to progress and achieve, and are more likely to attend university. On the other hand, there is increasing evidence that schooling itself has an impact on mental abilities. The most obvious examples of this are tests such as SATs and A-levels, which are designed to measure school learning. But it is also true of intelligence tests themselves: generally speaking, the more schooling you have, the better your IQ score will become.

This relationship has been shown in a variety of different ways over the years. For example, when children who are roughly the same age go through school a year apart because of birthday-related admission criteria, those who have been in school longer have higher mean scores.

Interruptions to school also have a detrimental effect. Children who attend school intermittently get lower IQ scores than those who go regularly. Amazingly, test scores even drop over the summer holidays when learning tends to be replaced by fun in the sun.

One famous example of this effect took place in the US state of Virginia in the 1960s. At that time, the schools in one county closed for several years to avoid integration, leaving many African-American children with no formal education at all. When researchers compared those children to their peers who had continued at school, their intelligence-test scores dropped by about six points for every year missed.

Schools can improve intelligence in several ways. The most obvious way is by teaching children new facts. Questions like 'What is the boiling point of water?' and

'In what continent is Egypt?' are typically learned at school – and are also included in IQ tests. But school also trains students in the type of thinking patterns that IQ tests reward, such as systematic problem solving, abstract thinking, categorisation and sustained attention. Miss out on school and you miss out on all these skills and your IQ will inevitably suffer.

How to help your child do well at school

- Read together: children who read at home with their parents perform better in school.

- Use TV wisely: academic achievement drops sharply for children who watch more than 10 hours of television a week.

- Establish a daily family routine with scheduled homework time.

- Keep in touch with the school and your children's teachers: do not wait for schools to tell you how your children are doing. Families who stay informed about their children's progress at school have higher-achieving children.

Cohabiting

+ 2 POINTS

Swedish researchers have found that people who live alone from midlife are almost three times as likely to develop cognitive impairment, including Alzheimer's disease, compared to those who live with a partner.

Researcher Krister Hahnsson and his colleagues started with the idea that remaining socially active can protect our precious cognitive functions. They reasoned that marriage, or other kinds of partnership, might be particularly important, considering the way they force us to adapt so regularly to another person's needs and perspectives. So they gathered data from a group of people in Finland over a period of more than two decades. At the end of the study, in 1998, 1,432 of the participants aged 65 to 79 were evaluated for signs of cognitive impairment.

From this group 139 people were diagnosed with cognitive impairment – 86 with mild impairment, and 53 with Alzheimer's disease. The study showed that those people who were not living with a spouse or partner were twice as likely to have some level of cognitive impairment later in life as those who were living with a partner. Those who lost their partner in midlife and did not remarry had the highest increased risk of cognitive impairment. Perhaps this points to the effect of combining psychological trauma with a lack of social and intellectual stimulation.

The researchers also reported that people with a genetic marker known as APOE-e4 – a risk factor of Alzheimer's disease – were particularly at risk if they were widowed or divorced from mid-life through late life. Those who were married and had the high-risk genotype were almost four times more likely to develop Alzheimer's, compared with a 25-fold risk to those who were divorced or widowed.

Loneliness

2 POINTS ▬

The great film-maker Orson Welles had this to say on the topic of loneliness: 'We're born alone, we live alone, we die alone. Only through our love and friendship can we create the illusion for the moment that we're not alone.'

Mr Welles was not perhaps the most cheerful man to win an Oscar, but his rather depressing quote does remind us of something fundamental about human beings – we crave companionship and suffer terribly when we lack it.

Not only does loneliness increase your risk of heart attacks, cancer and insomnia, but it also raises the chances that your hard-won mental faculties could slip away before you do. If you are looking for reasons to get out and make some friends, consider this: a recent study showed that people who are lonely in their old age are twice as likely to develop Alzheimer's disease as their socially active counterparts.

But how does socialising protect your cognitive function? Researchers suggest that getting out and about among friends and acquaintances probably forces people to communicate effectively and take part in complicated interpersonal exchanges. This challenging environment gets the mental cogs turning and sets in motion the adage 'use it or lose it' that helps you stay sharp into old age. Perhaps it's time to pick up the phone and arrange a catch-up?

Leaving work early

+ 0.5 POINTS

It's quarter to five on a Friday afternoon. You've worked hard all week, the sun is shining and escape is whispering your name. Your colleagues may be staring determinedly at their computers, lingering over an 'urgent' report due on Monday, but you grab your bag and run. Maybe you'll earn a black mark in the boss's book, but you know it's worth it. You're avoiding doing serious harm to your mental faculties.

Researchers who studied more than 2,000 British civil servants between 1997 and 2004 found that those who worked more than 55 hours a week suffered declines in their sharpness compared to those who called it quits after 40 hours a week. At the end of the study, the lingerers had noticeably lower scores in tests that measured memory, attention and speed of information processing.

The authors of the study point out that their findings could have medical significance, as the scale of decline seen in the overworked employees was similar in magnitude to that of smoking – a known risk factor for dementia. Considering how many of us do work long hours each week, this is bad news. In the European Union member states in 2001, for example, 12–17 per cent of employees worked overtime. Researchers have found that long working hours are linked to cardiovascular problems, reduced sleep and health problems such as diabetes.

Interestingly, although several of these factors are known to harm cognitive function, the study suggests that working long hours in itself is a separate risk factor. The bottom line seems to be that if you spend too long at work, it won't just be life that's passing you by… your mental powers could be slipping away too. So, isn't it time you headed home?

Napping
1 POINT

Staying at the top of your mental game during a long working day can be tough going. The good news is that taking a brief nap, even one that lasts just a few minutes, can make a world of difference to your cognitive abilities.

An Australian research team studied the impact of a 10-minute nap on the alertness and cognitive function of 16 healthy volunteers. They found that a brief kip left the participants noticeably more alert and better able to perform tests of their mental functions. The same research team found that the benefits of a 10-minute nap seemed to outstrip improvements after a 30-minute nap.

In a study in Japan, seven young adults found that a 20-minute nap in the afternoon improved their performance level and their confidence in performing tasks. Japanese researchers also showed that napping for 15 minutes improved logical reasoning. All this makes sense when you consider siestas, the midday rests that have long been part of the culture in many parts of the world, especially where the middle of the day is hot and sunny.

It might even be that we humans are naturally predisposed to getting our sleep in small snatches during the day. Solo sailors, who have to strive against the elements around the clock, tend to grab their sleep in chunks ranging from 20 minutes to 2 hours. Some other enthusiastic people have tried adapting their lives to this kind of schedule, sleeping at short intervals rather than in one period every day.

For those of us happy to get most of our sleep each night, the trick to successful napping seems to be ensuring you get enough sleep to rejuvenate yourself, without entering deep sleep that leaves you groggy afterwards. It is worth experimenting – naps can definitely sharpen up your afternoon.

Diabetes

— 1 POINT

Diabetes develops when the body does not make sufficient insulin or when the insulin that is produced does not function correctly. In type 1 diabetes, insulin-producing cells in the pancreas die. In the type 2 form, body tissues stop responding to insulin. In either case, the result is that our bodies become less able to regulate how much sugar is in the blood, which can lead to potentially deadly complications. It can also affect our mental functions in two important ways.

In the short term, the problems can arise due to episodes of low blood sugar, or hypoglycaemia. The symptoms of these episodes include headaches, weakness, irritability, mood changes, confusion and poor concentration. A US study of children, using a controlled hypoglycaemic clamp technique, showed that mental efficiency began to decline when blood glucose levels dropped.

In children whose diabetes began before five years of age, researchers have seen poorer cognitive performance and poorer school achievement. It may be that frequent and severe bouts of hypoglycaemia in early childhood contribute to these declines.

In the longer term, chronic high blood sugar predicts a mild decline in IQ scores and verbal IQ, suggesting that people whose blood sugar levels are continuously high may see their cognitive function decline.

The same link was seen in a study of British public servants published in 2005. Those with diabetes were approximately twice as likely to score poorly in a test of general intelligence compared to those who were not sufferers. However, other studies have suggested that not all aspects of intelligence are affected. One research group looked at all studies of cognitive function in people with type 1 diabetes and found evidence of a slowing of mental speed and diminished mental flexibility, but no effect on memory or learning.

Is there anything you can do to avoid these impacts? It might seem logical that the better you control your diabetes, the better you will do. Sadly, however, experts so far have yet to confirm whether this is the case. So until there are more positive results from such studies, the best thing you can do is try to prevent the likelihood of developing type 2 diabetes by ensuring you follow a healthy lifesyle.

How to avoid type 2 diabetes

Type 2 diabetes is the most common form of diabetes. Exactly what causes it is not completely clear, but there are known steps you can take to decrease the likelihood of developing it:

• Exercise regularly: aim for 30 minutes, five times a week.

• Try not to become overweight: obesity is found in approximately 55 per cent of patients, and even modest weight loss can make a difference.

• Stop smoking.

• Moderate your alcohol intake.

• Eat healthily: there is some evidence that wholegrain foods can help.

Silica in water

+ 0.5 POINTS?

Could the water you drink protect your mental sharpness by warding off Alzheimer's disease or other forms of dementia? There is growing evidence that the answer is yes, at least if that water contains the 'trace element' known as silica.

Silica is the most abundant mineral in the Earth's crust, so it's not surprising that it's also often found in water supplies. You might know it as sand, or quartz, or as the primary component of most types of glass. It plays an important role in your body in building connective tissue. And, it seems that the levels of silica in your drinking water correlate with the likelihood of your cognitive function declining as you age.

French researchers studied more than 7,000 women in five different parts of France, investigating the potential association between drinking-water composition and level of cognitive function. They found that the average amount of silica the women consumed varied dramatically – from 4 mg per litre, to 89 mg per litre of water. Those women whose cognitive function was normal drank more water each day, and consumed higher daily levels of silica from tap water and bottled mineral water. They then followed a subset of those women for up to seven years, and found a significant association between daily silica intakes and the later development of Alzheimer's disease. Women who developed Alzheimer's disease were almost three times more likely to have consumed less than 4 mg per day of silica.

The science behind this is still developing, so a full explanation of this link is yet to come. French researchers have suggested that silica might somehow protect against harm done by aluminium. But so far, the evidence against aluminium is too sketchy to say for certain. Meanwhile, other researchers have found that different elements present in drinking water, such as calcium, cadmium and zinc, could also have an effect on cognitive ageing. Perhaps it's time for a drink of water?

Heavy metal poisoning
3 POINTS ▬

You may have heard the phrase 'mad as a hatter'. It has its origins in a period of history when mercury was used in the process of curing felt for hats. As part of their work, hatters routinely inhaled toxic mercury fumes, and as a result developed symptoms such as confused speech and distorted vision. Mercury is known as a heavy metal – as are lead, arsenic and several other metals. When they enter the body they compete with essential minerals such as zinc, copper and calcium to interfere with normal organ functions.

Severe cases of heavy metal poisoning cause noticeable damage to brain function, especially if exposure happens in the womb, and these toxins can have an impact on cognitive functions at less obvious levels. Spanish researchers, for example, correlated levels of various metals in the hair of children with their ability to pay attention; they found there were notable differences in lead levels between children categorised as having medium- and high-attention levels.

And in 2008, US researchers found that children's intellectual functioning at six years of age was impaired by blood lead concentrations well below 10 µg/dL (micrograms of lead per decilitre of blood) defined by the US Center for Disease Control and Prevention as an elevated blood lead level.

Possible sources of heavy metal poisoning

- Dietary supplements. Metals are contained in some supplements.

- Food and drink stored in metal containers such as lead decanters.

- Colloidal metals taken for health benefits.

- Environmental contamination, such as industrial effluent dumped into water sources or lead paint.

Iron deficiency
2 POINTS

Iron deficiency is the most widespread nutritional problem in the world. An incredible 30 per cent of the world's population is anaemic, approximately half of which is attributed to iron deficiency (known as iron-deficiency anaemia). Among its many consequences are lower physical endurance, impaired immune response and poorer cognitive performance.

Public health experts know only too well the causes of iron deficiency. They include excessive menstrual bleeding or other blood loss, low dietary intake of the metal, problems with absorbing iron, and infections like malaria, HIV and tuberculosis. In any case, the damage can include noticeable behavioural changes, such as reduced attention span, lower emotional responsiveness and poor scores on tests of intelligence.

How to tackle iron deficiency

- Eat iron-rich foods such as red meat, poultry, oysters, fish, spinach and iron-fortified cereals and beans.

- Eat foods rich in vitamin C, such as oranges, when you eat iron-rich foods, as these help the body absorb iron.

- Check with your doctor before taking iron supplements.

- Cook in iron pots and pans.

- Avoid caffeine when eating iron-rich foods, since caffeine reduces iron absorption.

- Follow control programmes for malaria, hookworm and schistosomiasis to help control infection.

In childhood, the consequences can be long lasting. In one study of children in Costa Rica, those who had moderately severe iron-deficiency anaemia as infants had lower scores in tests of mental functioning at school entry. In the USA, a study of more than 5,000 children showed that even those with mild iron deficiency had worse maths scores. In severe cases, children can still suffer the developmental consequences more than 10 years later.

The good news is that iron deficiency is eminently treatable, and there is growing evidence that treating it can minimise its cognitive effects. Anaemic infants who are given iron supplements, for example, develop more quickly than those who do not receive supplements.

The benefit of treating low iron levels is not limited to children though. US researchers showed in 2004 that young women who took iron supplements for 16 weeks significantly improved their attention, short-term and long-term memory, and their performance on cognitive tasks, even though many were not considered to be anaemic when the study began.

Considering that approximately two billion people worldwide are thought to be affected by iron deficiency, treating it could have an enormous impact on mental sharpness on a global scale.

Creatine

+ 0.5 POINTS

Creatine is a natural compound that helps supply energy to muscle and nerve cells. Bodybuilders who want to increase their muscle mass take it as a supplement. For those of us interested in getting buff inside the skull, it might also be useful.

In one study, adult vegetarians who took 5 g (3 drams) of creatine powder per day for six weeks found that their working memory and overall intelligence scores improved compared to those who did not take the supplement. Volunteers given creatine were able to repeat back longer sequences of numbers from memory and had higher overall IQ scores. As the researchers said in their report, 'supplementation with creatine significantly increased intelligence compared with placebo'. What's more, it seems that creatine improves brain activity by providing extra energy for cognition.

Creatine supplements have also improved the cognitive performance of elderly people. Fifteen volunteers who took 5 g (3 drams) four times a day for two weeks showed a significant improvement in their ability in tests of spatial recall and long-term memory.

In another study, people who had been subjected to sleep deprivation for up to 24 hours demonstrated significantly less change in their reaction time, balance and mood state when given creatine. In all these situations, the added creatine may have been making up for a lack of it in the first place – vegetarians, for example, may have lower dietary intake of creatine than meat-eaters; and people deprived of sleep inevitably suffer diminished cognitive functions.

Research into the value of creatine reminds us of something it is easy to forget: that thinking requires energy.

Vitamin B12

0.5 POINTS? +

Vitamin B12 plays an essential role in the workings of the brain, and deficiencies can lead to serious and irreversible damage. Your levels need only drop slightly for you to be at risk of fatigue, depression and poor memory. This is a particular concern for the elderly – more than one in ten older people are deficient in the vitamin.

Recently, researchers have found that having good levels of vitamin B12 may protect older people from brain volume loss and reduce their risk of developing dementia. The study found that people with higher levels of the vitamin were six times less likely to experience brain shrinkage compared to people with lower vitamin levels.

Other researchers have shown that vitamin B12 levels are related to mental sharpness even within ranges that are considered normal. Unfortunately, studies have not shown conclusively that B12 supplements can improve cognitive function – some researchers have found no benefit, while others have found it can at least partly help. Until more results are forthcoming, experts suggest that the elderly in particular should be encouraged to maintain good levels of vitamin B12.

Food sources of vitamin B12

- Shellfish: clams, oysters and mussels are excellent sources of vitamin B12.

- Liver: the liver of almost any animal is bursting with vitamin B12.

- Caviar: fish eggs contain high levels of the vitamin.

- Octopus and fish.

- Beef and lamb.

- Dairy products such as milk and cheese.

- B12-fortified foods such as breakfast cereals, soy-based products and energy snack bars.

Ginkgo biloba

+ 0.5 POINTS?

The beautiful fan-shaped leaves of the ancient tree species *Ginkgo biloba* are the source of one of the world's most popular herbal remedies. Many people believe their concentrated extract can boost memory and concentration. In fact, ginkgo is widely used in several countries for treating dementia, where people believe it can improve blood flow to the brain, and for its antioxidant properties. There is also some evidence that ginkgo may improve thinking, learning and memory in people with Alzheimer's disease.

When it comes to boosting brainpower among the healthy, however, the results have been much less clear. In late 2008, for example, the largest trial to date on ginkgo showed that it was not effective in preventing or delaying the onset of dementia or Alzheimer's disease in people over 75. The GEM Study included more than 3,000 people who were followed for around six years – half were given ginkgo, half an inactive placebo. At the end of the trial, 523 individuals had developed dementia. Of those, 277 were receiving gingko and 246 were receiving the placebo. 'Based on the results of this trial, gingko cannot be recommended for the purpose of preventing dementia', the researchers concluded.

Other trials have shown that ginkgo may help improve thinking, learning and memory. In one UK study, researchers reported the supplement could produce a sustained improvement in attention in healthy young volunteers.

Overall, however, the results are mixed. Despite ginkgo's long history, the scientific evidence supporting its benefits remains questionable.

Eating regular meals
1 POINT

Starting the morning with a healthy breakfast and eating regular meals during the day are good ways to ensure you are in peak mental form. Skip meals and research suggests you could leave yourself struggling. On the other hand, a regular intake of food can improve your mood and leave you calmer, putting you in the right frame of mind for intellectual pursuits.

Eating regularly helps because it holds your blood glucose levels on an even keel. The brain is sensitive to short-term fluctuations in glucose supply, and there is evidence that keeping it steady can improve attention and reduce the effects of frustration. In fact, UK researchers have found that eating foods with a low glycaemic index – which means they release sugar into your bloodstream slowly – results in better cognitive performance in the hours that follow.

Research also shows that eating regularly benefits your short-term memory, improves rapid information processing, allows more focused and sustained attention—plus it helps you do arithmetic. It all adds up to a great way of sharpening your wits.

Low glycaemic index foods to keep your brain firing

- Oats, such as porridge or natural muesli.

- Multi-grain bread.

- Pasta.

- Low-fat milk and yoghurt.

- Most fruit.

- Salad with a vinaigrette dressing.

- Sweet potatoes.

- Legumes, such as beans or lentils.

43

Eating fish

+ 0.5 POINTS

Many of us grew up being told that fish is brain food. It turns out this old wives' tale was right on the money.

Many fish are rich in omega-3 fatty acids, oils that are essential for neurocognitive development and functioning. In fact, there are some researchers who suggest that modern human intelligence evolved in coastal regions because these oils were needed for brain growth.

Whether that is true or not, multiple studies in modern children and adults lend support to the benefits of eating fish. In 2006, for example, Harvard researchers studied 135 mothers and their infants, and found that the more fish the women ate during their second trimesters, the better their infants did on visual memory tests when they were six months old.

Italian researchers found that healthy people who supplemented their diet with omega-3 oils for just over a month experienced a boost in their attention compared to those given olive oil supplements. In another six-year study in Chicago, people over

the age of 65 who ate fish regularly tended to retain their cognitive functions longer. The rate of decline was slowed by around 10 per cent each year among those who consumed fish once or more times per week, compared with those who ate fish less regularly. Over six years, this added up to a difference of three to four years in brain age.

The only downside to eating fish – and it is a serious one – is that large oily fish tend to accumulate toxic levels of mercury in their bodies. Mercury has very negative health consequences and the US Government advises women of child-bearing age to avoid fish such as shark, swordfish or king mackerel.

Fish	Omega-3 fatty acids, grams per 85-g (3-oz) serving
Canned tuna (light)	0.17 – 0.24
Fresh tuna (bluefin)	1.4
Pollock	0.45
Salmon	1.1 – 1.9
Cod	0.15 – 0.24
Catfish	0.22 – 0.3
Flounder or sole	0.48
Crabs	0.27 – 0.40
Scallops	0.18 – 0.34
Herring	1.9 – 2.0
Sardines	0.8
Mackerel	1.1 – 1.7
Trout	0.8 – 1

Early onset of obesity

— 2 POINTS

In many countries around the world children are growing fatter. Early onset obesity is a problem that appears to be spiralling out of control, with potentially devastating health consequences such as diabetes, cardiovascular disease and asthma.

For adults, overweight and obesity ranges are determined by using weight and height to calculate a number called the 'body mass index' (BMI). BMI is calculated by dividing your weight in kilograms by your height in metres squared (or by dividing your weight in pounds by your height in inches squared and multiplying the figure by 703). An adult who has a BMI between 25 and 29.9 is considered overweight. An adult who has a BMI of 30 or higher is considered obese. BMI ranges for children and teens are defined so that they take into account normal differences in body fat between boys and girls and differences in body fat at various ages.

In 2006, US researchers reported that the brain can also be damaged by this condition. They found that children who became morbidly obese at a young age had lower results on intelligence tests and showed signs of lesions in their brains. They studied 17 children and adults with early onset morbid obesity – meaning they weighed at least one and a half times their ideal body weight before they were aged four – and 19 people with a condition called Prader-Willi syndrome, which is the most commonly recognised genetic cause of childhood obesity.

On average, both groups had significantly lower intellectual ability scores compared to their non-obese brothers and sisters. Prader-Willi patients had an average IQ of 63 and patients with early-onset morbid obesity had an average of 78. Their unaffected siblings had an average IQ of 106, which falls within the normal range.

The same research group also identified a possible explanation for the link between obesity and lower levels of intelligence. They saw lesions in the white matter of the brains of six children with Prader-Willi and five of those who were obese, compared with none among the 24 children of normal weight.

Although the work was preliminary, the researchers think that the damage was caused by the hormonal and metabolic imbalances that result from obesity. They also point out that children who become obese later in childhood are not at risk of cognitive impairment because their brains are sufficiently developed to fend off damage from obesity.

However, it is worth remembering that obesity can have a detrimental effect on a child's academic performance even without damaging the brain directly. Obese children are more likely to be the targets of social discrimination, and the pain and embarrassment inflicted by this kind of stigmatisation and teasing can have a terrible effect on a child's self-esteem. That in turn can do serious harm to a child's academic achievement and social functioning – with consequences that endure long into adulthood.

How to prevent your child from becoming obese

- Ensure children are provided with a choice of healthy foods.

- Familiarise your family with the five food groups and recommended amounts for each age group.

- Talk to your child about 'sometimes foods' and 'everyday foods'.

- Make physical activity part of every day.

- Limit 'screen time' of computer, television or other electronic games.

Eating animal fats

— 0.5 POINTS

Next time you wonder whether to have that bacon cheeseburger for lunch, consider this: the type of fat that dominates your diet seems to correlate with how sharply your mind functions. For example, children whose diets include a lot of cholesterol tend to do poorly when asked to remember strings of numbers. Researchers found in a study of more than 3,500 children between ages six and 16 that the more cholesterol they had in their diet, the worse they did in the test, which was used as a measure of 'working memory'. Students whose diet included poly-unsaturated fats from vegetables tended to do better on the tests.

There is evidence that the type of fats you consume can also affect your ability to stay sharp as you age. It seems that the more saturated fats you eat, the more likely you are to experience a decline in your mental faculties, while eating unsaturated fats offers protection. Some researchers have even found that high intakes of unsaturated, unhydrogenated fats may be protective against Alzheimers disease.

The connection between diet and the brain might seem mysterious until you consider that approximately 60 per cent of the brain comprises fats – particularly the omega-3, polyunsaturated, fatty acids.

What to eat for brain food

- Foods rich in omega-3, including: salmon, tuna, flaxseed and flax oil.

- Foods high in unsaturated fats, including: olive oil and avocado.

- Avoid foods high in saturated fats, including: meat, milk, fried foods, takeaway foods, pastries, biscuits, cakes and chocolate.

Blueberries
0.5 POINTS ✚

Research has shown that blueberries can improve your chances of maintaining a vital brain as you age. It seems that antioxidant pigments in blueberries (and similar berry fruits) can interfere with processes that lead to waning brain functions.

Researcher James Joseph and his colleagues have studied the benefits of blueberries in rats. First, they showed that feeding rats with dietary supplements of antioxidant fruits and vegetables for eight months slowed age-related declines in brain function. Then, in another study, they showed that rat-food pellets made with the antioxidant fruits – including strawberries, blueberries, spinach and kale – could actually reverse signs of ageing in 19-month-old rats. Testing each food separately, they found that the change was most dramatic in those rats that ate blueberries.

Examining the rats' brains, Joseph and his colleagues showed that the blueberries, and to a lesser extent the other foods, left the animals with healthier-looking brains. The membranes of the brain cells were more fluid and better able to move chemicals in and out, which probably improves how well the brain cells transmit messages. In particular, Joseph's team showed that blueberries have a positive effect on the hippocampus part of the brain associated with memory. Blueberry supplements improved the growth of cells in the hippocampus, and boosted levels of insulin-like growth factor-1, which is important in memory and learning.

Other scientists have shown that wild blueberries can protect brain cells from stroke-induced damage. After simulating the effect of a stroke in rats, they found that animals fed blueberries, in addition to their normal diet, lost less than half as many brain cells in their hippocampus as those who were fed no blueberries.

High blood pressure
— **1 POINT**

Taking steps to reduce high blood pressure could help you hang onto your mental faculties as you move into old age, because there is a very strong correlation between high blood pressure in midlife and levels of cognitive function in later life. The higher your blood pressure, the worse you fare.

About one in three US adults has high blood pressure, according to the American Heart Association – and because of it, they stand the risk of stroke, heart attack, heart failure or kidney failure.

Research shows that untreated high blood pressure (or hypertension, as doctors call it) is bad for the brain. In one study of almost 4,000 Japanese-American men living in Hawaii, every increase of 10 ml (0.3 fl oz) of mercury in systolic blood pressure increased the men's risk of poor cognitive function by

How to tackle high blood pressure

The Blood Pressure Association recommends a five-point plan to reduce blood pressure:

• Eat less salt. Don't add any to your food when cooking, and avoid salt-rich foods.

• Eat more fruit and vegetables: at least five fist-sized portions each day.

• Keep your weight down.

• Drink less alcohol. (See page 80 for recommendations and guidelines for responsible alcohol consumption.)

• Get more exercise. Being moderately active for 30 minutes each day can lower blood pressure.

9 per cent. Another study of 117 people between the ages of 45 and 75 found that those who maintained elevated systolic blood pressure throughout their lives were at increased risk of reduced verbal learning and memory function.

A third study, in British civil servants, showed that coronary heart disease – where there is poor circulation of blood and oxygen to the heart and surrounding tissue – was linked to poor reasoning and vocabulary later in life. That study suggested that even among middle-aged people, coronary heart disease is associated with poor cognitive performance.

Considering that growing numbers of people around the world are suffering coronary heart disease – in many Western countries it remains the leading cause of death – and that dementia affects more than one in three people over 80, it seems doubly sensible to do something about it. A few simple lifestyle changes that can make all the difference: stop smoking, lose weight and get some exercise.

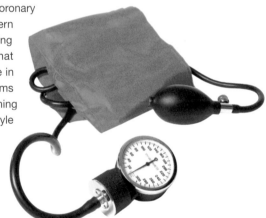

Eating tofu

— 0.5 POINTS

As a source of plant estrogens, tofu is regularly touted as a natural remedy for many of life's ills. But reports that have emerged in recent years suggest all may not be rosy in the world of the soybean. It appears that the brains of people who eat more tofu actually age more quickly than expected.

The first evidence of this worrying association emerged in 2000, when researchers examined men who had taken part in a study begun in 1965. By 1993, when the participants were aged in their 70s, 80s and 90s, those who had eaten the most tofu in midlife did worse on cognitive tests, had lower brain weight and showed greater signs of brain shrinkage. Among those who ate the most tofu, almost one in five showed signs of cognitive impairment, compared to less than one in 20 among those who ate the least. The same pattern was evident among their wives, who (presumably) ate roughly the same diet as their husbands.

In 2008, more evidence emerged. A study in two rural sites in Indonesia showed that people over 50 years of age who consumed more tofu – at least daily – tended to do poorly in a word learning test. Interestingly, those who ate a lot of tempe (a fermented whole soybean product) tended to have better memories. Fruit consumption also had a positive association.

These studies have left researchers scratching their heads. Plant estrogens may protect the brains of younger people, but in high quantities they seem to actually heighten the risk of dementia. One suggestion is that these molecules might promote the damage caused to cells by free radicals. Interestingly, tempe contains high levels of folate, which may protect against memory decline.

More research is needed to confirm the effect of tofu on the brain, but for now, its reputation is slightly diminished.

Eating your greens
0.5 POINTS +

The brain is a special organ: it requires a lot of metabolic energy and its cells are particularly long lived. Unfortunately, these characteristics leave the brain's tissue vulnerable to damage from free radicals – chemicals that react easily with other molecules. This may be why cognitive decline is such a common aspect of ageing.

Fortunately, many vegetables are high in antioxidants, molecules that counteract the damage done by free radicals. Several studies have shown that diets high in these vegetables can protect the brain. In 2005, for example, the Nurses' Health Study showed that among women over the age of 70, those who ate the most vegetables experienced a slower rate of cognitive decline than women who ate the least vegetables. Interestingly, fruit consumption did not appear to be associated with any change in cognitive ability. Other researchers, who studied a group of people aged over 65 in Chicago, found that the rate of cognitive decline among persons with the highest levels of vegetable intake was approximately 40 per cent slower than among those who ate the fewest vegetables.

Leafy green vegetables such as spinach, lettuce and chard are thought to be particularly beneficial, as are cruciferous vegetables, which include broccoli and cauliflower, although exactly what makes these vegetables so beneficial remains to be identified. One researcher has suggested that vitamin E in vegetables may be an important factor. Also, vegetables are often eaten with salad dressings, mayonnaise or butter, which can increase vitamin E absorption and other fat-soluble antioxidant nutrients, such as carotenoids and flavonoids.

Whatever the final verdict, it's a very good reason to follow Mum's advice… and eat your greens.

50

Smoking

— **3 POINTS**

Smoking not only increases the risk of serious health problems such as lung cancer, heart attack and stroke, it can also send your IQ up in smoke. It seems that smoking can have a negative effect on your cognitive functions.

In 2000, Scottish researchers assessed the mental faculties of 465 people who had completed an IQ test some 53 years earlier at the age of 11, in 1947. Approximately half of the volunteers were smokers at the time they were retested. They did considerably worse in five different cognitive tests than both the former smokers and those who had never smoked at all. The researchers found that overall, smoking appeared to cause a drop in cognitive function of just under 1 per cent.

In another study, US researchers found that smoking had an even more negative impact on mental function than alcoholism. They looked at 172 men from

How to quit smoking

Quitting smoking is good for your health and your intelligence. And if you don't succeed the first time, don't stop trying:

- S = Set a quit date.

- T = Tell family, friends and colleagues that you plan to quit.

- A = Anticipate and plan for the challenges you'll face while quitting.

- R = Remove cigarettes and other tobacco products from your home, car and work.

- T = Talk to your doctor about getting help to quit.

the same community – 103 of whom abused alcohol – putting them through a battery of tests that measured both IQ and thinking speed. They found that smokers performed the worst overall, and that the more the participants smoked, the worse their scores.

Interestingly, smokers often report that smoking a cigarette gives them a brief mental boost – perhaps reflecting the way our bodies come to depend on nicotine. Clearly, this benefit is reversed over the long term.

As for how smoking harms the brain, that is a question that remains to be answered. Researchers think it could be that the lung damage caused by smoking restricts the amount of oxygen getting to the brain. It might also be that the chemicals in cigarettes directly damage brain tissue.

Either way, the good news is that quitting seems to stop the rot. As the Scottish researchers showed, the effects of smoking on cognition were more evident in current smokers than those who had previously given up.

Drinking coffee

+ 0.5 POINTS

A steaming cup of coffee has long been a popular pick-me-up. So much so that we pour about 1.4 billion cups of coffee a day worldwide. That's a lot of coffee. In 2002, Norway topped the list of coffee consumers, averaging nearly 11 kg (24 lb) of coffee per person per year, with Finland and Denmark close behind. The caffeine contained in the drink acts on certain receptors in the brain, helping to stave off drowsiness and heighten alertness.

Research suggests that coffee, tea or other drinks containing caffeine might be just the thing if you need to be mentally alert. Scientists have shown that drinking as little as a single cup of coffee can have a significant impact on alertness.

In one recent study, Canadian researchers found that even people who were regular coffee drinkers – and therefore might be expected to be 'immune' to the effects of coffee – experienced a lift.

'Whether you are hooked on caffeine or not, if you need a boost, coffee improves your mental alertness and can have a calming effect on your heart rate,' said researcher Michael Kennedy of the University of Alberta.

In another study, Australian researchers gave drivers a capsule containing 200 mg of caffeine, roughly equivalent to two cups of coffee, or a dummy substance. Those who received the caffeine had improved reaction times and alertness that persisted for about three hours. Too much coffee and caffeine is of course bad for your health, but it seems that a cup or two can give you a mental boost.

Marijuana

1 POINT   –

Smoking marijuana or cannabis interferes with the harmonious workings of the brain, dulling the areas responsible for short-term memory and attention. Cannabis can also have a negative impact on IQ. In one study, heavy smokers experienced a decline in their IQ scores of four points in the course of a decade.

Interestingly, it looks as if those who have the least to lose, IQ-wise, tend to do worse. One US study showed that people with a lower IQ experience a more profound impairment than those who began with a higher IQ. Whether these effects on IQ linger once people stop using the drug is not clear-cut. Some researchers think that an IQ drop can right itself once people stop smoking; although research suggests that those who take up cannabis smoking at an early age – while the brain is still developing – may lose something they can never get back.

Exactly why this should be so is not clear. It might be that early-onset smokers have lower cognitive skills before they started smoking marijuana or that young marijuana users neglect school and so miss out on learning certain cognitive skills.

The most worrying possibility is that marijuana itself has a toxic effect on the developing brain. As things stand, there is little direct evidence that this is the case for moderate users – but the latest research shows that heavy, long-term cannabis use can trigger minor structural abnormalities in the brain.

53

Ecstasy

— 0.5 POINTS

People take the illicit drug Ecstasy because it delivers them briefly into a euphoric world, free of fear and anxiety. But users might not feel so cheerful when they learn that the drug may damage nerve cells involved in mood, thinking, learning and memory.

Dutch researchers probed the effects of Ecstasy on intelligence by following a group of young adults, none of whom had yet used the drug, but all of whom thought they would probably give it a try in the near future. At the beginning of the study they asked each participant to take tests of their memory – including attention, verbal memory and the ability to remember images. Over the following three years, 58 of the participants did begin using the drug, so the researchers asked them to retake the memory tests. They then compared the results with repeat test scores from 60 participants who hadn't tried the drug.

At the beginning of the study, all the study participants had roughly the same test scores, but after three years of taking the drug, users were significantly less able to recall words they had been asked to remember. The advantage of this trial was that it was able to study people before and after they began taking the drug – and see what happened in comparison to not taking the drug.

The results of this study and others suggest that Ecstasy affects mainly verbal memory, indicating that specific brain chemicals may be affected by the drug. The main impact seems to be a depletion of a signalling molecule called serotonin, which is involved in learning and memory. Something worth remembering the next time someone offers you Ecstasy.

Alcoholism

2 POINTS   ▬

A couple of drinks a day might be good for your cognitive function, but too much becomes harmful. Between 45 and 70 per cent of people entering treatment for alcoholism have specific deficits in problem solving, abstract thinking and memory, among other things. Although these problems might not be detectable without specific tests, researchers have shown structural changes in the brains of alcoholics and reduced blood flow to the brain.

Roughly one in ten severe alcoholics experience serious brain impairments, such as alcohol-related amnesia and dementia. A study of elderly Canadian people found that alcohol abuse among people over 65 is associated with cognitive impairment. On the positive side, there is some evidence that the cognitive impairments seen in some alcoholics might be reversible if they quit. Among non-alcoholics, the results are not conclusive; some research shows that the more you drink the lower you are likely to score on certain tests. Other studies have shown no such connection.

How to cut down on your drinking

- Keep track of your consumption so that you can clearly see how much you are drinking.

- Set daily and weekly limits.

- Socialise away from the pub. Catch up with friends at a coffee shop.

- Alternate a glass of alcohol with a glass of water. Never take an alcoholic drink to quench your thirst.

- Try low-alcohol alternatives: wine spritzers or low-alcohol beer.

Alcohol in moderation

+ **1 POINT**

When it comes to alcohol and intelligence, less is definitely more. Overindulging in alcohol is unquestionably bad for your body and your brain; but research has also shown that sensible and moderate drinking might actually improve brain function.

Guidelines to healthy drinking

- The UK Government recommends women drink no more than two to three units of alcohol a day, and men drink no more than three to four units. (One unit is 10 ml (¼ oz) of alcohol, which is equivalent to a 0.5 l (1 pt) of standard strength beer, or a half standard glass of wine.)

- In the US, men are advised to consume no more than two drinks per day, and women no more than one drink. (A standard drink is defined as 350 ml (¾ pt) of beer (one bottle); a 150 ml (5 fl oz) glass of wine; or 45 ml (1.5 fl oz) of 80-proof distilled spirits.)

- In Canada, men and women are advised not to exceed two units per day (27.2 g (1 oz) of alcohol per day).

- In Denmark, men are advised to limit intake to no more than 21 alcohol units a week, and women no more than 14 units.

- In Japan, the Ministry of Health, Labour and Welfare recommends a daily limit of one to two units per day (where a unit is 19.75 g (¾ oz) of alcohol).

- In Australia, new recommendations recommend that more than two drinks a day is a health risk.

In 2000, researchers in Tokyo tested the IQ of 2,000 people between the ages of 40 and 79. Men who drank less than 540 ml (1 pt) of sake or wine a day had an IQ 3.3 points higher than men who did not drink at all. Similarly, women drinkers scored 2.5 points higher than teetotallers.

The Japanese team pointed out that their findings did not suggest that everyone should suddenly take up drink. For one thing, it may be that people who drink moderately have other advantages that are responsible for the higher IQ – such as better nutrition.

However, the evidence in favour of moderate drinking is still accumulating. In the USA, researchers found that women who drink up to one standard drink a day may be at lower risk of cognitive decline as they age. Others have shown that low alcohol doses improve problem-solving capability and short-term memory.

More recently, New Zealand researchers have studied the positive effects of alcohol on memory, showing that in rats moderate doses of alcohol had a beneficial effect on signalling between brain cells in a part of the brain known as the hippocampus, which plays an important role in the formation of memories.

When it comes to physical fitness, we all know you need to exercise if you want to stay on peak form. We also know that you must practise your skills if you want to get better at your favourite sport. After all, nobody ever won Wimbledon without a lot of hard work and rigorous training. But what about mental fitness? Does exercising the brain boost your intellectual prowess?

For many years, experts were uncertain about the benefits of mental workouts. This was partly because most scientists believed that once childhood had passed, the brain lost the capacity to grow new cells or connections. Nowadays, that notion has been over-turned. Sophisticated brain imaging techniques have shown that the adult brain has the ability to change. Most importantly, like the muscles in your arms and legs, it responds to training.

The question now is what kinds of exercises make a real difference? What should you do to defend yourself against dementia? Are there any activities that can boost your IQ score? And, on the other hand, are there things you should avoid doing because they harm the brain? Researchers are currently probing these very questions. And although the science in this area is relatively new, some solid answers are emerging. The bottom line? Yes, the things you do every day, from taking a walk to eating regular meals, can affect your mental sharpness for good or ill.

PART THREE

Activities

Brain training

➕ 2 POINTS

Is it really possible to increase your overall intelligence with brain-training exercises? Until recently it seemed that the answer was no. Any training you did simply improved the skill you were utilising. (If you wanted to improve your scores on intelligence tests, the best way was to practise the tests.)

But in April 2008, Swiss and US researchers showed for the first time that a specific kind of memory test could have a positive impact on overall 'fluid intelligence' – the element of intelligence that allows us to adapt our thinking to new problems or situations. Fluid intelligence draws on the ability to understand relationships between various concepts, independent of any previous knowledge or skills. The research shows that this part of intelligence can be improved through memory training.

Researchers gathered four groups of volunteers and trained their working memories using a complex task called 'dual n-back training,' which presented both auditory and visual cues that participants had to temporarily store and recall. In the task, participants were shown a series of white squares in different positions against a black background on a computer screen. Simultaneously, they heard a voice reading out single letters. Their task was to remember whether the letters spoken and box positions were the same as those they had heard and seen two, three, four, etc., items before.

Participants received the training during a half-hour session held once a day for either 8, 12, 17 or 19 days. For each of the training periods, researchers tested participants' gains in fluid intelligence. They compared the results against those of control groups to be sure the volunteers had improved their fluid intelligence, not merely their test-taking skills.

The results showed that control groups made gains over time, presumably because they had practice with the fluid intelligence tests. But the trained groups improved considerably more, and the longer the participants trained, the larger were their intelligence gains.

The findings clearly show that training on certain memory tasks transfers to fluid intelligence, the researchers said. There is every likelihood that improved fluid intelligence scores could translate into improved general intelligence as measured by IQ tests.

So instead of regarding fluid intelligence as an immutable trait – as many have done – these new results provide evidence that, with appropriate training, it can be improved.

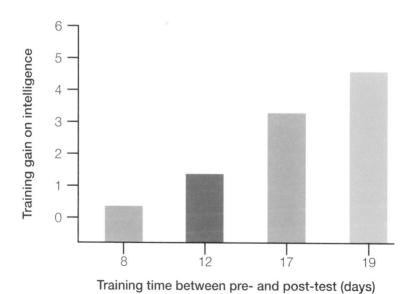

Training time between pre- and post-test (days)

Head Start programme

+ **1 POINT**

Since 1965, more than 22 million pre-school-aged children in the USA have participated in a programme called Head Start, which provides education, nutrition, health and parent-involvement services to low-income families. Forty years after the programme began, a report was ordered by Congress to examine its impact.

The report assessed a random selection of 5,000 children who at age three or four had entered either a Head Start programme or a similar service their parents had chosen. It found that the programmes had a moderate but noticeable impact on several different areas of the children's developing cognitive function. The most positive impact was the children's emerging reading skills and their parents' views on how their literacy and language was developing. The children also showed improvements in pre-writing and vocabulary.

Another study within Head Start looked at longer-term results and found that children who took part in the study were more likely to finish high school and attend college and significantly less likely to have been charged or convicted of a crime.

Not all researchers are so enthusiastic about the programme, with some saying that any gains made in the programme are lost if the children are then put into disadvantaged schools. However, overall, the fact that the Congressional report compared outcomes between children who were randomly assigned to Head Start or a similar programme makes its results pretty believable, suggesting Head Start may well offer children a foot up onto the educational ladder.

Brain games

0.5 POINTS? +

Computer games designed to give your mental powers extra zip, ward off dementia and boost your memory are big business, but are they effective? A lot of people certainly think so. In scientific terms there is positive evidence, too, although it's not conclusive.

The games can be played on hand-held consoles or on games platforms that run through the television. They present a variety of timed challenges that are intended to combine fun with a mental workout. The concept is compelling. There is no doubt that being mentally active throughout your life reduces the risk of developing dementia. The question is whether brain-training games improve overall mental 'fitness' or whether they simply train you to be better at brain-training games.

In one study, researchers, sponsored by the producers of a computer-based brain fitness system, found that after 10 weeks of training for an hour per day, participants improved their ability to recall a sequence of sounds. Research of another computer-training programme demonstrated that people who used it for 20 minutes every few days for 24 sessions improved in a range of cognitive measures.

In a longer-term study, healthy older people who used computer-training programmes to target specific skills – memory, reasoning or speed – did better in those skills five years later. Meanwhile, in Scotland, pupils who played a brain-training game on a hand-held game system each day for nine weeks did better in maths than other children.

These games are unlikely to provide a miracle cure for dementia. In fact, it may be that computer brain games are no more effective than exercises using pen and paper. But if they are more fun, perhaps there may be more incentive to do them.

Mnemonics

1 POINT

Organising the mess on your desk can make life easier when you are trying to find an important file or document, and the same principle applies when it comes to organising your memory.

One trick that people have been using for centuries to help them remember things is the mnemonic – poems, words, sounds or movements that create easily remembered connections to help organise related information. This is based on the idea that the average person finds it much easier to remember an actual phrase or personal, meaningful information than to recall pieces of random information.

Some popular mnemonics

- Every Good Boy Deserves Favour – the order of the treble clef in music: E, G, B, D, F.

- Brass – for how to shoot a rifle: Breath, Relax, Aim, Sight, Squeeze.

- Big Elephants Can Always Understand Small Elephants – how to spell 'because'.

- Never Eat Shredded Wheat – the order of points on the compass: North, East, South, West.

- King Phil Classed Ordinary Families as Generous and Special – the taxonomic order in biology: Kingdom, Phylum, Class, Order, Family, Genus, Species.

- My Very Easy Method: Just Set Up Nine Planets – the names of the planets in order of distance from the sun: Mercury, Venus, Earth, Mars, Jupiter, Saturn, Uranus, Neptune, Pluto.

The most popular type of mnemonic device are words or phrases made up of the first letters of the information you are trying to commit to memory. For example, remembering the names of the planets in order of their distance from the sun is easy when you use the phrase My Very Easy Method: Just Set Up Nine Planets – Mercury, Venus, Earth, Mars, Jupiter, Saturn, Uranus, Neptune, Pluto.

Another ancient type of mnemonic involves creating a Memory Palace. To do this, you visualise yourself walking a series of parts of a familiar building. To memorise a speech, you break it up into sections and symbolise each section with an image. Place each of those images into different parts of the building, so that you can now recall those thoughts in order as you imagine walking through the building.

There is another type of mnemonic system, called the phonetic number system, which works by converting numbers into consonant sounds – and then into words by adding vowels. Words are more easily recalled than numbers, especially words that are visual and emotive.

Critical thinking

✚ 0.5 POINTS

If you want to do a good job of evaluating a new situation, you need to think carefully and clearly about the facts in front of you. In other words, you need to think critically. Training yourself to think this way can help hone your cognitive skills towards a desired outcome.

Training yourself to think critically helps improve your judgment. It is about carefully evaluating what to believe or do in response to things you see, read or hear. Organisations such as the military and medical schools try to inculcate students with critical thinking skills to help them approach complicated situations with more clarity.

Critical thinking can improve your academic performance by helping you understand the arguments and views of others, evaluate those arguments and views, and develop your own perspective. This is distinct from simply absorbing facts as they are presented; instead you are evaluating and applying the understanding you gain from the information you have been given.

Tips for developing critical thinking

- Be sceptical: do not accept things at face value; think them through.

- Focus on the facts: rather than blindly following theories, focus on data, and analyse what the information tells you.

- Emphasise the important: focus your energy on things that matter.

- Be wary of group thinking: understand the influence the beliefs of others has on views formed by your own experience.

Playing computer games
0.5 POINTS? +

Many parents worry that computer games will rot their children's minds, but new research suggests otherwise. Games might actually be making kids smarter!

Social critic Steven Johnson, author of the book *Everything Bad is Good for You*, says video games force children to manage multiple objectives at the same time. They also require gamers to complete a number of tasks to win and prioritise their actions – both of which stimulate 'fluid intelligence' or problem solving.

Some experts say that the more sophisticated media world our children are growing up in has been a factor that contributes to rising IQ scores around the world – a phenomenon known as the Flynn effect. Certainly, some games develop just the type of skills that are challenged in IQ tests.

So perhaps games are not all bad – at least not the less violent types. Perhaps by letting children spend a moderate amount of time in a virtual universe, we are helping them with the type of decision-making they are going to need in the real world.

Listening to music

+ 0.5 POINTS

In 1993, the idea that listening to Mozart could boost your intelligence gained a great deal of attention after researchers found that 36 college undergraduates improved their ability to mentally manipulate objects in three-dimensional space after listening to 10 minutes of a sonata written by the great composer. Suddenly, the 'Mozart Effect' was born, spawning a veritable industry of recordings that promised to boost intelligence.

In the years since that first report the conclusions of the original research have often been overstated. Researchers who tried to repeat the initial study failed to get the same results. Others have reviewed a wide range of different studies and found that overall the impact of listening to Mozart was not significant.

And yet, there are many researchers who still believe that listening to music can enhance your overall cognitive arousal and your ability to concentrate. One Belgian group, for example, found that a music-based exercise programme could improve cognitive function in a group of women with dementia.

In 2006, researchers reported in the Annals of the New York Academy of Sciences that listening to any music you find enjoyable has positive effects on cognition. The study actually found that the spatial abilities of 10 and 11 year olds

improved when the children were allowed to listen to pop music, but not when they were played Mozart. So if you happen to enjoy Mozart, by all means play his music. If you don't, perhaps sticking to what you like might be more effective.

Playing an instrument
1 POINT +

Picture a glorious summer's day in childhood. The sun is shining; all your friends are outdoors kicking a ball around. There's nothing you'd rather do than run out and join them but you can't. Mrs McGinty is sitting beside you at the piano, waiting to hear you bash through Mozart, again. Why, oh why?

Well, here is why: over the past few decades, the evidence that music makes you smarter has built to a crescendo. Whether you tinkle the ivories, slide the trombone or flaunt your skills on the flute, learning and practising a musical instrument in childhood appears to stimulate cognitive development and build skills in a range of areas.

In one study, 144 six-year-olds were assigned to music lessons, drama lessons or no lessons; those in the music groups showed greater increases in IQ. The effect was relatively small, but still, it was there.

In another study, children who had already taken three or more years of music lessons did better on tests of their verbal ability and in non-verbal reasoning. The longer they had been playing the instrument, the better they did.

Some researchers suggest that music lessons act as extra schooling – demanding that children focus their attention, memorise notes and master technical skills. On the other hand, it could be that the skills you learn in music help with specific non-musical tasks: for example, learning to decode musical notation might help you read. It may also be that music training boosts brain circuitry.

Either way, there is really no excuse for not practising!

Early exposure to TV
− 0.5 POINTS

Television entertains us, informs us and connects us to a wider world. It is part of an increasingly rich cultural background that could be contributing to increases in intelligence worldwide. But what effect does television have on the minds of children? There is some evidence that for very young children watching television can have a negative impact on their subsequent development.

In 2005, researchers reported on a study of the effect of watching television on the intellectual abilities of US children before the age of three years, once they had reached six or seven. Their study included more than 5,000 children who were aged six in the 1990s. They found that children watched an average of 2.2 hours of television a day under the age of three. Between the ages of three and five, they watched more than three hours a day.

For each hour of television watched before age three, children did progressively worse on tests of reading and memory. The impact was 'modest'. Nevertheless, the impact was strong enough for them to recommend that children younger than two years of age should not watch television.

Watching television in early childhood might also lead to attention problems, other researchers have found. They looked at 1,200 children aged three years and 1,300 children aged five years. For every hour of television watched per day at those ages, their chance of having attention problems by the time they reached seven had gone up on average by almost 10 per cent.

But the impact does not seem to stop at age three. In New Zealand, a study of 1,000 children born in the early 1970s, and followed up when they were 26 years old, showed that every hour of television watched in childhood and adolescence (up to age 15) was associated with a higher chance of leaving high school without qualifications and a lower chance of attending university.

Not all experts agree with the findings of this research, but given what's at stake, it might be worth following the 'better safe than sorry' advice of the American Academy of Pediatrics. The first two years of life are especially important in the growth and development of a child's brain. During this time, what children need is good, positive interaction with other children and adults – television is no substitute for that interaction.

Tips for cutting down on TV viewing time

- Create a TV schedule: select what programmes to watch or set a daily limit on screen time. Try to set a good example by limiting your own TV time as well as theirs.

- Replace TV time with family activities, games or reading.

- Switch off during meal times.

- Remove the TV from children's rooms.

- Encourage children to engage in other interests. Keep plenty of games, toys, books, puzzles and magazines as other fun options.

- Get out of the house: go for a picnic or a family walk.

Playing chess
✚ 0.5 POINTS

People have been playing chess (or a form of chess) for over a thousand years. For most of that time, great chess players have been regarded as paragons of intellectual ability. Although the rules of the game are simple, there is something awesome about the strategic thinking required to play the game well. So much so, that for a long time computer scientists who were trying to build 'intelligent' computers would measure their success by whether the computer could beat humans at chess.

These days, research into artificial intelligence has moved onto different challenges, such as building a computer that can hold a conversation, and the link between chess and intelligence has moved on too. Researchers have evidence that playing chess can actually make you smarter.

In school-based studies around the world, from Zaire to Texas, researchers have found that regularly attending Chess Club can help children improve their reading, maths and other aspects of thinking.

Some chess masters argue that playing the game helps develop general intelligence, self-control, analytical skills and concentration. Others disagree, saying that learning to do well at chess boosts a student's self-belief. So the answers, unlike the chessboard itself, are far from black and white.

Learning a new skill
2 POINTS

One of the most profound observations made by scientists in recent times is that adult brains are more adaptable and capable of change than was once thought.

Rather than being fixed and unchanging organs that can only decline as time passes, our brains are capable of adapting to changing circumstances, giving birth to new cells and new connections. Give the brain something new to grapple with and it will make new connections.

In the USA, one of the most significant studies to look at developing cognitive functions in older people is called the ACTIVE trial: Advanced Cognitive Training for the Independent and Vital Elderly trial. In that trial, researchers gave training in mnemonics, reasoning and speed-of-processing to nearly 3,000 people over the age of 65. They found that the training exercises delivered cognitive improvements that lasted for at least two years.

The trick to building new neural circuits seems to be novelty. In 2008, UK researchers suggested that when people learn new skills like playing the piano or riding a bicycle, new brain cells become wrapped in insulating sheets known as myelin, bringing into play pre-formed brain circuits that were previously wired but that were not yet fully functional.

As psychologist K. Warner Schaie told *The New York Times* in 2008, 'Another thing that's important as people get older is to maintain flexible attitudes and be willing to try new things. You have to expect things will shift over time and won't be the same as when you were young.'

Roll with the punches, enjoy change, challenge your brain. You won't regret it.

Becoming a taxi driver

+ 0.5 POINTS

London taxi drivers' brains grow on the job. Well, parts of them do, at least.

According to studies by scientists at University College London published in 2000, professional drivers have a larger posterior hippocampus, the region of the brain tied to learning and navigation.

The hippocampus, which is located on the bottom of the brain, and is shaped a little like a seahorse (it gets its name from the Greek word for the creature), plays a major role in short-term memory and in spatial navigation. The researchers found that part of the hippocampus is larger in taxi drivers than in the general public, and that the more experienced drivers have bigger hippocampi.

It seems likely that by using that part of their brain strenuously to remember how to navigate around the city, taxi drivers are building their hippocampus in much the same way as bodybuilders work on their biceps.

Still, there may be a downside. As brain regions continually compete for space, the growth of the posterior hippocampus in the taxi drivers seems to come at the cost to the anterior hippocampus, which is associated with memory.

Meanwhile, it is not only taxi drivers who can beef up their hippocampi. German scientists reported in 2006 that the brains of medical students, while studying for final exams, showed increases in the posterior hippocampus. Three months later, the hippocampi had returned to their former size.

68

Learning another language
1 POINT +

Learning another language is obviously useful when it comes to finding the train station in a foreign land, but a wealth of research also suggests it has more fundamental benefits to your mental abilities.

A study of sixth-grade students in the USA who learned French showed that those who learned for 30 minutes a day for two years did better on tests that involved evaluating new information, which is considered a high-level cognitive skill. In another study, 18 English-speaking six-year-olds who attended a French language immersion programme had higher IQ scores than a group who attended a comparable English programme.

Experts say that learning another language can be thought of as a cognitive problem-solving activity. Many studies have shown that learning a foreign language increases critical thinking skills, creativity and mental flexibility in young children.

Researchers have also found that these benefits seem to apply to children who are bilingual. In one study of almost 100 five- to eight-year-olds, those who were bilingual in Hebrew and English had more advanced skills in processing verbal material and more discriminating perceptual distinctions than children with only one language. Similarly, a Swedish study of children from Stockholm who were bilingual in Swedish and Persian found that they did better on tests that assessed their memory.

Perhaps the benefits of learning more than one language come from the need to organise the information of two languages. It may also help in the understanding of the way language works. Bilingual children seem to develop analytical thinking about language.

Learning another language brings these benefits, so what are you waiting for? On y va! Avanti! Let's go!

Being creative

+ **2 POINTS**

Intelligence is about much more than vocabulary, memory and comprehension. According to the 'triarchic intelligence' theories of researcher Robert J. Sternberg, it also includes creative and practical elements.

Sternberg argues that analytical abilities can help us to evaluate, analyse, compare and contrast information. Creative abilities add invention and discovery to the mix. Practical abilities tie everything together by allowing individuals to apply what they have learned in the appropriate setting. 'To be successful in life the individual must make the best use of his or her analytical, creative and practical strengths, while at the same time compensating for weaknesses in any of these areas,' he writes.

Sternberg and his colleagues argue that creativity is an essential component of learning and problem solving. 'Virtually any problem, by the virtue of definition, imposes on its solver some ambiguity that needs to be overcome.'

Another popular way of thinking about the links between intelligence and creativity is called 'the threshold hypothesis'. This idea, proposed by Ellis Paul Torrance, holds that a high degree of intelligence is necessary but not sufficient for a person to have a high degree of creativity.

Whichever way you think about the associations between intelligence and creativity, encouraging your own creative attitude and skills is an important part of intelligence.

Crafts

1 POINT +

Pick up your needle and thread, or throw a lump of clay onto the wheel: crafts like pottery and quilting have joined the list of activities that can help reduce your risk of memory loss in old age. Scientists from the Mayo Clinic in Minnesota studied 197 people between the ages of 70 and 89 who either had signs of mild cognitive impairment or who had been diagnosed with memory loss. They compared them with another 1,124 people in the same age bracket who had no signs of memory problems.

Both groups were asked to describe their daily activities within the past year and in middle age, when they were between 50 and 65 years old. During their later years, those who had done craft activities such as pottery or quilting, or other mentally stimulating activities, had a 30 to 50 per cent lower risk of developing memory loss than people who did not do those activities.

Those people who participated in crafts and social activities during middle age were also about 40 per cent less likely to develop memory loss than those who did not do those activities. 'By simply engaging in cognitive exercise, you can protect against future memory loss,' said study author neuropsychiatrist Dr Yonas Geda.

More research is probably needed to confirm the results, Dr Geda said – partly because the study relied on past memories of the participants, which may not be completely accurate.

Still, the findings, first presented at a scientific meeting of the American Academy of Neurology, reinforce the idea that you don't have to take the ageing process sitting down. Exercising your grey matter throughout your life can affect how sharp you are in old age.

Gardening

✚ 2 POINTS

If you want a sharp brain, cultivate green fingers. Getting your hands dirty in the garden could help you stay mentally fit as you age. Australian researchers followed nearly 3,000 people over the age of 60 for 16 years and found that daily gardening reduced their risk of developing dementia by 36 per cent.

The 'Dubbo Study', which began in 1988, included only people who were free of any impairments to their mental faculties at the beginning of the study. The researchers found that 56 per cent of men and 41 per cent of women gardened daily. They even found that gardening less than once a week offered some protection against dementia.

The potential benefits of gardening for the brain are easy to imagine. As an activity it provides exercise, stress relief and a creative outlet, all of which are known to have positive mental impacts. In addition, gardens provide an excellent supply of the fresh fruits and vegetables that are needed for a healthy diet.

Learning philosophy as a child

1 POINT

If your mental image of a philosopher is a grey-bearded man who spends his days pondering his navel, then think again. Around the world children in primary schools are being taught a philosophical approach to thinking, with some remarkable effects on their intelligence.

One particular programme for teaching philosophical skills is called Philosophy for Children. It was developed in the 1970s by US psychologist Matthew Lipman and his colleagues. The idea is that students and teachers share a short story, a picture, a poem or an object, and use it as a stimulus for discussion.

The children raise different questions and then select one for more intensive discussion. The teacher's job is to encourage the children to welcome the diversity of each others' views and to use them as the start of a process that involves questioning assumptions, developing opinions and reasoning.

In 2003, a group of Scottish researchers evaluated ten of these programmes to see what impact they had had on the abilities of children. All the studies showed positive outcomes in terms of reading, reasoning, cognitive ability and self-esteem.

When the researchers combined the data, they found there was a consistent effect that suggested an average gain in IQ of 6.5 points for each child.

So if you think of philosophy as something far removed from everyday life, think again. When you consider that IQ scores tend to predict how well you will do in school or the type of job you will have, these results make philosophy seem very practical indeed.

Reading a book

+ 2 POINTS

Learning to read and write is the cornerstone of education, and it is easy to see how failing to acquire these fundamental skills could harm your ability to do well in life. But does learning the written form of a language affect brain function itself? The answer seems to be yes.

Thanks to advances in medical technology, it is possible these days to study what goes on in the brain while we are thinking. Techniques like PET scans and fMRI allow researchers to study the blood flow and energy use in different parts of the brain when people are asked to do specific mental tasks.

In the late 1990s, European researchers performed one such study on a group of people who were illiterate, requiring them to repeat a series of real words and made-up words.

The results showed that different parts of the brain became active when the illiterate people repeated the made-up words, compared to literate people. The research suggests that learning to read and write helps shape the structure of the brain. Other studies have shown that the effects of formal schooling are not limited to language-related skills. They also seem to affect our ability to work with shapes.

These results seem to correlate well with studies that have looked at the impact of reading and writing on intelligence. As one scientist said, if smarter means having a larger vocabulary, more world knowledge and better abstract reasoning skills, then reading does seem to make people smarter.

Meditation

0.5 POINTS +

Meditation has been a central part of many religions for thousands of years, offering followers a way to calm their minds and get a little closer to enlightenment. More recently, researchers have been subjecting the practice to scientific scrutiny and have begun to find that meditation has benefits beyond its spiritual roots. Not only does it foster calm and contentedness, they have found it can help make you smarter.

The aim of meditation is to focus your mind on a single thought or point of reference. Proponents say that doing this regularly is a little like fitness training for the brain.

In fact, even as little as 30 minutes of meditation a day can boost your focus and mental performance. After just eight weeks of mindfulness training, volunteers who had not meditated before experienced improvements in their ability to focus and keep their attention at the ready.

Other research has suggested that people who meditate regularly are better at sustaining their attention for long periods of time compared to the general population. The more meditation practice you have, the better your concentration.

Wherever you are – at school, in a meeting or watching television – the ability to concentrate is crucial to learning. Considering meditation also lowers the blood pressure and can foster happiness, sitting quietly has never looked so appealing!

Physical exercise

+ 2 POINTS

Although it can be tempting to think of our minds and bodies as separate things, it is worth remembering that the brain is an organ that is affected by what goes on in the rest of the body. That is why it makes perfect sense that exercise has been shown to have a positive effect on mental sharpness.

In early 2009, for example, Canadian researchers looked at the effects of fitness levels on women over 65. They found that active women had significantly better cognitive function scores. Australian researchers, meanwhile, showed that volunteers who had memory problems, but not dementia, saw a modest improvement in their memory after six months of physical activity. The improvements lasted for the length of the 18-month follow-up period.

How to incorporate exercise into your daily life

- Work in the garden or mow the grass. Rake leaves, prune and dig.

- Take a short walk before breakfast and after dinner.

- Park further away at the shopping centre and walk the extra distance.

- Walk or ride your bike to work or the shops rather than driving.

- Plan holidays that involve physical activity such as hiking or swimming.

- Take up a activity such as tennis, golf or dancing.

- When travelling, stay in hotels with gyms – and use them.

- Take the stairs instead of the escalator.

The implication of these and other studies is that exercise might help offset some of the mental declines that are associated with the ageing process. Exactly how it might do so is not clear. One factor might be blood flow. Exercise in general improves the heart's capacity to pump blood and improves the blood's oxygen-carrying capacity. It might be that exercising improves blood flow to the brain.

Interestingly, a review of the evidence linking exercise and cognitive function published in early 2008 noted that the improvements in cognitive function that can be attributed to exercise might not be due to improved fitness. There are other ways in which exercising might affect your mind. For example, it can get you out, and encourage socialising, both of which have been shown to have a positive impact on mental sharpness. Exercise can also help combat depression, which might be another way it helps. In other words, you have got nothing to lose and plenty to gain by getting a little exercise, for your mind's sake.

Dancing

+ 2 POINTS

If exercise in general is good for the brain (see page 106), then dancing seems to be particularly good. Not only does it keep you fit, it also exercises your grey matter.

When US researchers studied the link between a host of different leisure activities and the risk of dementia in a study of senior citizens, dancing came out on top. In the 21-year study, people who danced regularly were, on average, 76 per cent less likely to develop dementia.

Dancing not only exercises the body, it also places demands on the brain. In one study, older people who took tango classes saw greater improvements in balance, posture and motor coordination than those who simply walked. The tango dancers also performed better at a complicated cognitive task while walking.

It could be that the mental effort involved in dancing – remembering steps, making split-second, careful adjustments to your movements and so on – stimulates the ability of the brain to make new connections between brain cells. The brain only does this when it needs to – when it is challenged.

There is another benefit, too: dancing is almost always a social activity. As Swedish researchers noted, social networks themselves can protect against cognitive decline and dementia.

To sum up, an active and socially integrated lifestyle seems to protect against dementia by stimulating you mentally, exercising you physically and connecting you socially. Dance offers all three benefits in one package.

Yoga

1 POINT

The combination of breathing, movement and meditation that makes up yoga practice helps calm the mind and exercise the body. There is also some evidence that it can improve cognitive functions such as memory.

In 2008, for example, Indian yoga experts looked at the effect of yoga therapy on cognitive abilities in women who were suffering hot flushes and other symptoms of menopause. They divided 120 women into two groups – half practised a daily set of breathing exercises, sun salutations and cyclic meditation, while the others did a set of simple physical exercises for an hour a day, five days a week for two months.

At the end of the study, the women in the yoga group had fewer hot flushes and night sweats and less sleep disturbance, but they also saw improvements in cognitive function such as remote memory, mental balance, attention and concentration, delayed and immediate recall, verbal retention and recognition.

Yoga has also been shown to offer benefits to school children. In another Indian study, researchers compared memory tests for two groups of children aged between 11 and 16. One group of 30 children went to a yoga camp, while the other group went to a fine arts camp. Both groups were assessed before and after the 10-day camp. A control group of 30 children who didn't do any special activities were also measured.

The yoga camp included regular practise of physical postures, yoga breathing, meditation and guided relaxation. At the end of the camp, the yoga group showed an increase of 43 per cent in their spatial memory scores, the researchers found. The fine arts and control groups showed no change.

Tai chi

+ 1 POINT

The slow, graceful movements of people practising the traditional Chinese martial art of tai chi are becoming a familiar sight in parks and other public places around the world. With roots that stretch back hundreds of years, this ancient form of exercise claims numerous health benefits, and these in turn have direct and indirect effects on cognitive functions.

In general the physical activity involved can help combat the effects of ageing on mental sharpness (see page 106), but more specifically, there is some evidence that practising tai chi can bring cognitive benefits for older people. In one study of 132 healthy older adults, for example, US researchers compared Western and Eastern modes of exercise over the course of a year.

For a start, those who were randomly assigned to tai chi had greater improvements in balance, adding seven seconds to a single-leg stance test, compared with their scores at the beginning of the study. The Western exercise group added four seconds.

As well as studying a number of physical aspects such as balance, the researchers also compared cognitive function between the groups, using tests that asked them to name different animals and to recall strings of digits. On the test that asked participants to recall strings of numbers in reverse order (a test that is thought to assess attention, concentration and mental tracking), the tai chi group's score went up an average of 0.6 points in the course of the study, while the average score went down 0.7 points in the Western exercise group.

Other researchers have found that tai chi can help people who are already suffering the effects of dementia. They have found that those with early stage dementia can slow their physical, mental and psychological decline by taking part in programmes that combine tai chi with counselling and support groups.

Nursing professor Sandy Burgener and colleagues asked 24 people with early stage dementia to participate in an intensive 40-week programme. The intervention included sessions of cognitive behavioural therapy and support groups every two weeks, plus three sessions per week of traditional Chinese martial arts exercises and meditation, called qigong and tai chi. For comparison, they asked another group of people with early stage dementia to not participate in these programmes for the first 20 weeks of the intervention.

After 20 weeks, those in the treatment group improved in several measures of physical function. There were also positive cognitive and psychological effects, including gains in self-esteem and modest improvements in mental status scores, which were maintained after the study ended.

Boxing

— 2 POINTS

Common sense might suggest that a sport that involves being repeatedly punched in the head is likely to do your brain some harm, and scientific evidence confirms that boxing can cause long-term damage to mental faculties.

Professional boxers who undergo multiple bouts and repeated head blows are prone to a condition doctors call chronic traumatic encephalopathy (CTE). This results from the shaking of the brain within the skull and causes problems such as tremors and Parkinson's disease, plus cognitive changes such as mental slowing and memory deficits.

Doctors have a technical term to describe the effects of repeated head trauma experienced by boxers – they call it dementia pugilistica or punch-drunk syndrome. Examining the brains of boxers reveals tangles of neural fibres together with the kind of plaques that characterise Alzheimer's disease.

The condition is thought to affect around 15 per cent of professional boxers. Football players can also experience the same effects if they experience blows to the head.

Interestingly, there seems to be little evidence to suggest that amateur boxers, who wear protective head gear, suffer chronic traumatic brain injury. In 2007, researchers examined 36 different studies and found that fewer than one in four of them found any indication of chronic traumatic brain injury, and then only a minority of amateur boxers.

Taking a walk

1 POINT

Help for your failing memory could be just a stroll away. Australian researchers found that walking for two and a half hours a week can significantly improve memory problems in the over-50s.

That study, reported in 2008, shows that moderate exercise can positively affect cognitive function. Crucially, the scientists found that the improvement in memory occurred not only during the six-month trial, but also continued for up to a year afterwards.

The trial included 170 people who had reported memory problems but did not meet the criteria for dementia, divided into two groups. One group continued their usual activities, the other took part in a 24-week, home-based, physical activity programme with the aim of walking three 50-minute sessions or other moderate exercise each week. Participants in the exercise group did an average of 140 more minutes in a week, or 20 minutes in a day, than those in the control group.

By the end of the study, participants in the exercise group performed better on cognitive tests and had improved recall time. Their mental function was measured using a test specifically designed to assess possible Alzheimer's disease.

That same year, US researchers added a twist to the benefits of taking a constitutional stroll. A University of Michigan team showed that a walk in the woods improved short-term memory by 20 per cent, while walking in an urban setting did not. In this case, the benefits seem to have come from the ability of nature to restore your powers of concentration.

Consider for a moment your brain. We've all got one, but for many of us it remains a mystery. The average human brain weighs roughly 3 lb (1.5 kg) and contains a whopping 50 billion cells or thereabouts. That much is easy enough to measure. But how do our thoughts, feelings, memories and sense of self actually emerge from that dense tangle of neurons? Those are some of the most profound questions we have to answer about what it means to be human.

At a more specific level, the same kinds of questions apply to intelligence. Are there particular characteristics of our brains that make one person smarter than another? Characteristics that make one person better at languages or maths or dancing than another? Tentative answers to these questions are now emerging as researchers seek to correlate intelligence with attributes such as the speed with which brain cells deliver messages, brain size and so on.

The next question is whether we can do anything to boost the brain's power. Some people are already using brain drugs to try and boost their attention, memory and mental sharpness. Perhaps in the future, gene therapy, stem cells or other technological wizardry will do even more. Such advances might seem like science fiction, but they may be less remote than you think.

PART FOUR

The brain and its future

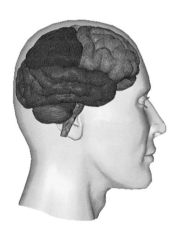

Grey matter

+ **1 POINT**

People who do better in IQ tests seem to have more grey matter in specific parts of their brain, according to US researchers who conducted a comprehensive structural brain-scan study in 2004.

As you might have been told in school biology classes, brain tissue is divided into two types: grey matter and white matter. Grey matter is made up of the cell bodies of nerve cells. White matter is made up of the long filaments that extend from the cell bodies, the 'wires' that transmit electrical messages between neurons.

Californian researcher Richard Haier and colleagues used a technique called magnetic resonance imaging (MRI) to map the brains of 47 adults who also took standard IQ tests. They found that their IQ scores were related to a range of different areas of grey matter in different parts of their brains and that various different combinations of areas could account for IQ scores.

It is therefore likely that a person's mental strengths and weaknesses depend in large part on the individual pattern of grey matter across their brain.

Interestingly, although grey matter volumes were strongly linked to intelligence scores, the researchers found that only about 6 per cent of all grey matter in the brain is related to IQ. Still, the fact that IQ scores correlated to the amount of a particular type of brain tissue suggests that IQ tests really are measuring physical differences in brain abilities.

White matter
1 POINT

In 2004, US researchers found that the amount of grey matter in the brain seemed to correlate to IQ scores (see page 116). A year later, they found that the volume of white matter was important too – at least in females.

Their study found significant differences in brain areas between males and females. Intellectual skill related to white matter volume in women and grey matter volume in men.

Grey matter represents information processing centres in the brain and white matter represents connections between these processing centres.

The study showed that women had more white matter and men more grey matter related to intellectual skill, revealing that no single structure of brain anatomy determines general intelligence and that different types of brain designs are capable of producing equivalent intellectual performance.

Generally speaking, men have about six times as much grey matter related to general intelligence than women, and women have nearly ten times the amount of white matter related to intelligence than men.

Richard Haier, who led this work, suggests that human evolution has created two different types of brain designed for equally intelligent behaviour – one for women and one for men.

The results might also explain why men and women tend to have different intellectual strengths. Men tend to excel in tasks requiring more local processing, such as maths, while women tend to excel at integrating and assimilating information from distributed grey-matter regions in the brain, as required for language facility.

Small brain

2 POINTS

When it comes to intelligence, it could be that bigger is better. A growing body of evidence suggests that, to some extent, people with larger brains really do seem to be brainier.

In 2005, for example, US researcher Sandra Witelson tested the intelligence of 100 neurologically normal, terminally ill volunteers, who agreed that their brains could be measured after death. They found that people with bigger brains were more intelligent, but that there were differences between women and men.

In women, verbal intelligence was clearly correlated to brain size, accounting for 36 per cent of differences in verbal IQ scores. In men, however, this was only true for right-handers, suggesting that brain asymmetry is a factor in men.

Spatial intelligence was also correlated to brain size in women, but less strongly. In men, spatial ability was not related to overall brain size. These results suggest that perhaps women use verbal strategies in spatial thinking, but that in men, verbal and spatial thinking are more distinct.

In fact, Witelson's study is just one of many that have linked smaller brain sizes to lower scores on intelligence tests. US researcher Michael McDaniel, for example, combined the results from 37 studies, including data from 1,530 people, and found a strong correlation. For all age and sex groups, it was clear that brain volume was positively correlated to intelligence.

Fast brainwaves

1 POINT

For much of human history, the inner workings of the brain have been a mystery, and to a large extent they still are. But scientists now have tools at their disposal that allow them to probe the brain when we are thinking. What they have found is that the way the brain works correlates with your intelligence.

Firstly, the brains of people with higher intelligence scores tend to react more quickly to images, sounds or other stimuli. The less time a person needs to make an accurate decision on an obvious stimulus, the higher their IQ.

In 2001, Dutch researchers analysed this correlation and found that it was entirely due to a common genetic factor. Their suspicion was that the genetic link had to do with the process of wrapping nerve cells in a protective sheath known as myelin.

Two years later, another group of scientists made an important contribution to our understanding of how brain activity relates to intelligence. They used a technique known as functional MRI (fMRI) to monitor the brain activity of volunteers as they did a series of more or less challenging tests of their working memory.

They found that activity in a part of the brain known as the pre-frontal cortex (which scientists think is involved in reasoning and novel problem solving) made the difference. Higher intelligence was related to higher activity in that part of the brain.

Interestingly, the volume of grey matter in the pre-frontal cortex is strongly controlled by genetics, which makes sense considering other studies have found that intelligence levels are partly genetic.

Energy-hungry brain

— 1 POINT

The first time you set out to try a complicated new task, such as putting together flat-pack bookshelves, the likelihood is that you will struggle a little, sweat and most likely bang your thumb with a hammer before finally managing to erect them. The next time you do it, it is a little easier. You expend less energy. You are more efficient.

So it seems to be with the brain. Each time your brain sends a message, it uses energy to do so. But it seems that in learning to do a mental task, you also learn which parts of the brain you need for a job and stop 'wasting' energy on the mental equivalent of flailing around with pieces of wood and a screwdriver. As you learn to perform a complicated mental task, the amount of energy your brain needs to accomplish it diminishes.

When scientists compare people with lower and higher IQs, they generally find that sharper people have more efficient brains. They use less energy to perform the same task. In fact, German researchers have shown that people with higher IQ scores gain much greater efficiencies in brain exertion after they learn something than people with lower general mental abilities. The opposite also seems to be true: the harder a person's brain works during some tests, the less well they tend to solve the problems.

Brain injury
3 POINTS —

More than 11 million people in the USA and Europe are currently thought to be living with the ramifications of a traumatic brain injury. The consequences include disabling cognitive, behavioural and personality problems.

Even apparently minor brain injuries can cause harm. Among the most common impairments are difficulties with memory, mood and concentration. Others include a reduced ability to organise and reduced reasoning skills. Researchers have been trying for years to develop treatments for these problems, but the complex biochemical and neurological pathways triggered by brain injuries have proven more than a match for their ingenuity. Nevertheless, while there are currently no drugs for this indication, there are reasons to hope that this situation will be remedied in the future. The mechanisms of what happens immediately after an injury are becoming better understood and the search for drugs is becoming more focused. Some experts hope that over the next five to ten years there will be a significant breakthrough. Some of the new developments will be in gene therapy, others will be pharmacological and there are also likely to be new surgical techniques.

How to avoid brain injury

- Wear a helmet when riding a bicycle and motorcycle: bike accidents are a major cause of brain injury.

- Wear your seatbelt: many cases of brain injury come from motor vehicle accidents.

- Be careful around electricity: electric shocks can lead to brain damage.

- Protect yourself when involved in contact sports, such as boxing.

Stroke

— 2 POINTS

When a blood vessel in the brain bursts or becomes blocked, causing a loss of brain function, it is known as a stroke. The damage that results can be permanent and strokes are among the leading causes of disability in the developed world.

The cognitive deficits resulting from stroke include perceptual disorders, dementia and problems with speech, attention and memory. In long-term outcomes, the impact of strokes also depends on other variables. In one study, scientists followed 193 patients for two years after their stroke to see if they could identify the factors that related to cognitive decline. They found that in almost 80 per cent of cases, the patients' cognitive status had stabilised within two years. In 8 per cent, some of the harm recorded soon after the stroke had actually improved. However, in 14 per cent of patients, the decline continued. Older people, those who had signs of mental decline before the stroke, and those who were taking several different medicines were most likely to suffer ongoing decline, as were those who suffered episodes of low blood pressure during their stay in hospital.

How to identify someone having a stroke

Use the 'FAST' clues to identify someone having a stroke:

- Facial weakness: can the person smile? Has their mouth or eye drooped?

- Arm weakness: can they raise both arms by themselves?

- Speech difficulty – can they speak clearly and understand what you say?

- Time to act fast – call an ambulance immediately.

Fast nerves

1 POINT

The brains of people with high IQs are equipped with faster nerves, researchers have found. It seems that the speedy cells deliver messages more quickly, allowing information to be processed more quickly.

Researcher Arthur Jensen and others have conducted several experiments that show a link between IQ and nerve velocity in brain nerve pathways. In one of the first such tests, Jensen and colleagues gave 147 university-level students IQ tests and then measured the speed of a nerve pathway in the visual part of the brain. They found a strong correlation.

In other studies, researchers have looked at the relationship between intelligence scores and decision-making time in so-called 'elementary cognitive tasks'. These tasks are so simple that adults and most children can do them accurately in less than a second. In one of the tests, the subject is asked to react when a light goes on by lifting their index finger off one button and immediately depressing another button. The researchers take two measurements: the number of milliseconds between the light going on and the subject lifting their finger off the home button (called the decision time); and the number of milliseconds between the subject's release of the home button and pressing of the response button (called the movement time).

Studies showed that movement times are unrelated to intelligence, while the decision times of people with higher IQs are slightly faster than those of people with lower IQs. As the tasks are made more complex, correlations between average decision times and IQ increase.

Thick cerebral cortex

+ 1 POINT

Very intelligent children seem to have brains that develop in distinctive ways. Their cerebral cortex – the folded outer layer of the brain involved in complex thinking – starts thin and grows thicker.

Researchers scanned the brains of approximately 300 healthy children between the ages of six and 19. All the children had their brains scanned once, many were scanned twice and more than 90 were scanned three times at different points in childhood. The scans showed that children with the highest IQs began with a relatively thin cortex that quickly grew thicker, before peaking and becoming thinner again. Children of average intelligence had a thicker cortex around age six, but by around 13 years it was thinner than in children of superior intelligence.

Researchers have long known that the cortex thins in late adolescence, perhaps because the brain prunes neurons and connections that are not being used. But the study found that the cortex continued to thicken in gifted children until around age 11 or 12, much later than in children of average intelligence. The results do not necessarily mean that anyone's intellectual destiny is set in stone at birth. Just the opposite, in fact. Because the cortex is highly malleable, experience and environmental cues may play a very important role in shaping intelligence.

As UK researcher Richard E. Passingham noted at the time the research was published: 'It could be that people with superior intelligence also live in a richer social and linguistic environment, and that it is this that accounts for the sharp increase in the thickness of their prefrontal cortex in late childhood.'

Does having a thick cerebral cortex in adolescence make you smart? Or does the intelligence that comes from a rich environment give you a thick cerebral cortex? For now, those are questions without answers.

Epilepsy

0.5 POINTS —

Epilepsy is the collective name for the seizures that result from unprovoked storms of electrical activity in the brain. About 50 million people worldwide are thought to have epilepsy at any one time.

The effects of epilepsy vary, depending in which parts of the brain the seizures originate from, but there is growing evidence that in the long term the condition has a damaging effect on cognitive function. The negative effects seem to be greatest in people whose epilepsy begins early and continues uncontrolled for many years.

Among people with temporal lobe epilepsy, two studies showed that epilepsy that did not respond to treatment seemed to induce a very slow but ongoing deterioration in cognitive function. Researchers think that the impact of epilepsy on the brain exhausts the capacity of brain functions.

In 2003, German researchers also found that chronic temporal lobe epilepsy was associated with progressive memory impairment. However, they noted that memory decline may be stopped and even reversed if seizures are fully controlled.

What to do if someone has a seizure

Most seizures stop safely in a few minutes, but there are things you can do to help:

- Do not put anything in the patient's mouth. People having seizures do not swallow their tongue.

- If the seizure does not stop within several minutes, call an ambulance.

- Once the seizure stops, position the patient on their side to prevent food or fluids being breathed into the lungs.

Phenylketonuria

— 0.5 POINTS

Anyone who has paid close attention to the side of a can of diet cola may have spotted a little warning: 'Not suitable for phenylketonurics'. This is an important message, because phenylketonuria is a condition that can lead to irreversible mental retardation unless treated. The treatment? Avoid consuming an amino acid called phenylalanine, which is found in many things we eat and drink.

People with phenylketonuria are born with a deficiency in an enzyme called phenylalanine hydroxylase, which breaks down phenylalanine into other essential compounds in the body. When the enzyme does not do its job properly, phenylalanine builds up.

The trouble is that excessive levels of phenylalanine significantly decrease the levels of other amino acids in the brain. Because these amino acids are needed to build the proteins and molecules that brain cells use to communicate, the disease disrupts brain development.

The good news is that phenylketonuria is one of the few genetic diseases that can be controlled by diet. In the developed world, babies are tested for the condition at birth. Those found to have phenylketonuria are put onto a diet low in protein, which is an effective treatment.

Some people, however, stop the low protein diet once they are through childhood. In 2006, UK researchers looked at the cognitive effects of this switch. Their study of 25 patients who discontinued their diets in adolescence and 25 adults who stayed on their diet, showed that the group who stayed on the diet had slightly higher levels of ability at remembering lists of numbers.

Magnetic stimulation
0.5 POINTS

The specialised cells that make up our brains and nervous system communicate with one another via a type of relay system of electrical impulses. That is why doctors sometimes use electroconvulsive therapy on some people with serious mental illness to try and 'reset' the brain.

Recently, a less invasive technique has been developed, called transcranial magnetic stimulation, in which researchers place an insulated electromagnetic coil on the patient's scalp to generate magnetic field pulses that are roughly as strong as a routine MRI scan. These pulses pass unhindered through the skull, where they stimulate an electric current in the underlying neurons.

Researchers have recently shown that the technique might also be useful for staving off declines in brain function that come from lack of sleep or old age. In one study, for example, researchers from Columbia University were able to partly counteract the effects of 48 hours of sleep deprivation by using this approach. In another study of 20 Spanish elders with memory deficits, ten 10-second bursts of the magnet improved their ability to perform memory challenges compared to 20 similar people who had a sham procedure.

Neurodegeneration

— 3 POINTS

Whichever way you look at it, your ability to think sharply is a function of the brain. It stands to reason that anything that causes damage to the brain could have an impact on those functions.

Neurodegeneration, the progressive loss of the structure or function of brain cells, is the mechanism behind several different brain conditions, including Alzheimer's disease, Parkinson's disease and Huntington's disease.

At first glance, the causes of the degeneration in these conditions seem to vary quite significantly, but as researchers examine them more closely, it seems that there are links at the level of genes and molecules involved. Research into the molecular causes of these diseases has now progressed far enough that researchers are translating their research results into clinically relevant outcomes.

In 2009, for example, researchers led by scientists from the Mayo Clinic discovered a genetic defect that results in profound depression and Parkinsonism in a disorder known as Perry syndrome. This syndrome is exceedingly rare, but the mechanism implicated in it may help explain the origins of a variety of neurodegenerative disorders, such as Parkinson's, amyotrophic lateral sclerosis and even common depression and sleep disorders.

'Understanding why distinct neurons are selectively vulnerable to neurodegeneration in different brain disorders is one of the greatest puzzles in neuroscience,' said lead investigator Matthew J. Farrer. 'These findings suggest that trafficking of specific cargoes inside brain cells may be a general problem in a variety of neurodegenerative diseases, depression and other disorders.'

As research into these common links develops, scientists are hopeful that the declining cognitive function associated with some neurodegeneration can be stopped and perhaps even reversed.

Concussion

2 POINTS —

A left hook to the side of the head, a crunching tackle in football, a dramatic tumble in the school playground. There are lots of ways to suffer concussion and they all leave you momentarily dazed. But do they cause permanent damage? The latest research suggests they do.

After comparing 19 healthy former college-level hockey or football players who had sustained a concussion more than 30 years earlier with 21 former athletes with no history of concussion, researchers concluded that the injury can have lasting effects on the sharpness of the mental faculties. Even those who had been concussed only once or twice in their 20s or 30s showed a decline in their attention and memory.

Importantly, the former athletes in this study were not suffering any of the major effects of repeated concussions, such as punch-drunk syndrome, the type of dementia that affects boxers (see page 112). The cognitive changes they experienced were minor and did not affect their everyday life. Still, the results raise questions about whether sports concussions might be accelerating the ageing process. If so, then there could be serious implications as the athletes grow older. Increasing age is the most potent risk factor of Alzheimer's disease.

Grades of concussion

- Grade 1: Confusion, symptoms last less than 15 minutes, no loss of consciousness.

- Grade 2: Symptoms last more than 15 minutes, no loss of consciousness.

- Grade 3: Loss of consciousness.

Nanobots

+ 3 POINTS?

The American inventor and thinker Ray Kurzweil has said that he can envisage a time within the next few decades when microscopic robots will be implanted into our brains to make us more intelligent.

Kurzweil has himself been called the ultimate thinking machine. He specialises in imagining what the future will be like and has a particular interest in artificial intelligence. In an interview reported on *BBC News*, he said: 'We'll have intelligent nanobots go into our brains through the capillaries and interact directly with our biological neurons.'

Nanobots are hypothetical microscopic robots built from small numbers of molecules. Smaller than a red blood cell, they will theoretically be able to enter the body to perform therapeutic functions and boost the capabilities of our bodies and brains. According to Kurzweil, nanobots will 'make us smarter, remember things better and automatically go into full emergent virtual reality environments through the nervous system'.

In fact, the intelligence-boosting bots would be just part of a wider merging of humans and machines with human-level intelligence that could happen as soon as 2029, Kurzweil said. 'Its really part of our civilisation. I've made the case that we will have both the hardware and the software to achieve human-level artificial intelligence with the broad suppleness of human intelligence including our emotional intelligence by 2029.'

Although nanobots are currently in the realm of science fiction, researchers have already begun to understand how to use groups of molecules to make these tiny machines. Who knows, they could be the building blocks for brain-boosting robots of the future.

Artificial intelligence
5 POINTS +

Machines that can think have been the essence of science fiction for centuries. There are some people who think that the day will come when individual humans are able to supplement their own intelligence with artificial smarts using artificial intelligence technology.

But the challenge of creating human-like learning and abilities in a computer has proven greater than many in the field ever imagined. In 1965, for example, scientist Marvin Minsky claimed that 'Within a generation... the problem of creating "artificial intelligence" will substantially be solved'. Sadly he was a little off the mark, although since the 1990s researchers have made important breakthroughs. These days, success in solving some of the difficulties in creating 'intelligence' has translated to applications in medical diagnosis, speech recognition and perception.

Where this leaves us in the future is anyone's guess. Some researchers argue that it is not a question of 'if' robots can match human intelligence, but 'when'. Some even say machines will outstrip human-level intelligence by 2030 or sooner. Other thinkers envisage a time when these super-intelligences could be directly linked to our own flesh and blood, blurring the boundaries between 'real' and 'artificial' intelligence. If it becomes possible to link humans to these 'artificial' intelligences in some way, then we could become unimaginably more intelligent ourselves. Some of these theorists think of themselves as 'transhumanists' and believe that humans can and should use technologies, such as artificial intelligence, to become more than human.

Supplemental brains

2 POINTS

Steve Mann, a professor at the University of Toronto in Canada, has sometimes been called the world's first cyborg (a human-machine hybrid). Mann has been experimenting with information from computers to add to or subtract from what he sees in the world around him, giving him 'mental' capacities he would otherwise lack.

For more than 20 years, Mann has worn a web of wires, computers and electronic sensors to augment his memory, enhance his vision and keep tabs on his vital signs. Information from the computer is projected onto the spectacles he wears and in this way, his view of the world is modified by the computer. If he sets the computer to grey-out certain advertising billboards, he does not see them. If he uses a face-recognition programme, the computer can remind him of the person's name each time he sees them. The computer is a supplement to his brain. In other words, the computer systems he wears enhance aspects of his own intelligence.

The connection between Mann's biological brain and the supplemental data from his wearable computer has become something he cannot manage without. In 2002, *The New York Times* reported that he suffered badly when airport guards insisted he detach himself from his equipment to pass through security and he lost the use of his vision system and computer memory. The experience left him unable to concentrate and behaving differently. 'He is now undergoing tests to determine whether his brain has been affected by the sudden detachment from the technology,' the newspaper reported.

The systems that Mann and others wear are built from technology that any of us could choose to wear. Perhaps as technologies advance, they will become less obtrusive and more socially acceptable. Just as people now can use 'bionic ears' or cochlear implants to enhance their hearing, maybe one day we will all use bionic brains to enhance our mental functions.

Brain drugs

1 POINT

As researchers learn about the detailed biological processes that power our brains, the possibility of enhancing them with drugs is becoming a reality. In the future, a longer memory, sharper mind or better attitude may be just a pill or two away.

There are several companies already at work in this area. Cortex Pharmaceuticals, for example, has developed drugs that amplify brain-signalling processes that are involved in memory, attention and learning. Human trials of their drugs are already underway and have shown early signs of promise. Meanwhile, Memory Pharmaceuticals is developing drugs to combat dementia. One of its drugs modifies calcium channel receptors in brain cells, allowing information to be transmitted more speedily. Another modulates a type of nicotine receptor that plays a role in synaptic plasticity. Both apparently improve memory.

Another company, Targacept, is also working on nicotinic receptors and has drugs in development for Alzheimer's disease, among other conditions. These companies hope to cure the memory deficits that come with ageing, but if these compounds can fix deficient memories, then they may be able to enhance normal memories as well.

Drugs that could enhance brain power

- Piracetam: claims to enhance cognition and memory, slow brain ageing and increase blood flow and oxygen to the brain.

- Aniracetam: purports to be more potent than Piracetam.

- Ritalin: said to improve focus and memory.

- Provigil: promotes wakefulness in patients with sleep disorders. Some people use it to replace sleep.

Genetic engineering

+ 3 POINTS

Every part of our body, including our brain, is built and operated according to instructions laid down in our genes – parts of the DNA molecules present in most of our cells. Given this, it makes sense that genes have an impact on brain functions. In fact, it turns out that – in mice at least – careful alterations to genes can lead to improvements in memory and intelligence.

In 1999, for example, researchers made one of the first 'smart' mice by tweaking their genes to produce a specific form of a molecule that helps attract calcium into brain cells. The modified form of that molecule, known as the N-methyl-D-aspartate (NMDA) receptor, results in an enhancement of the signalling between brain cells that serves as the basis for enduring memories.

More recently, researchers showed that removing the gene for a protein called cyclin-dependent kinasE 5 (Cdk5) improved memory performance in mice. The technique interfered with Cdk5's normal role in breaking down NMDA receptors. By 'knocking out' the Cdk5 gene, the researchers made mice that were more adept at learning and more able to quickly decipher environmental changes. Interestingly, this gene has been implicated in the development of Alzheimer's disease in humans, so understanding how it affects the brain and behaviour might help to develop new treatments. Other researchers made their own variety of smart mouse by genetically reducing the activity of a protein called $eIF2\alpha$, which normally suppresses the transfer of memories from short term to long term.

Of course, genetically manipulating humans and mice are two very different things, and nobody is suggesting (yet) that gene therapy should be used to make humans smarter. But the knowledge these studies are yielding could lead to drugs that target these particular processes. If that happens, treatments for dementia and other conditions could be the result.

Stem cells

2 POINTS +

Stem cells are master cells that have the ability to develop and differentiate into many of the different types of cells that our bodies need. For example, there are stem cells in bone marrow that can develop into different kinds of blood cell, and there are stem cells in the brain that researchers have found might serve a useful purpose in improving cognitive function.

In one experiment, US researchers injected human brain stem cells into the brains of two-year-old rats. They found that cells were extensively incorporated into the rat brains, leading to an improved ability to navigate a standard test called the Morris water maze. Because two-year-old rats are considered to be elderly, the results suggested that human brain stem cells could be used to generate replacement cells for those lost as a result of neurodegeneration.

Other researchers bred a strain of mice that progressively lost brain cells in the hippocampus, a part of the brain involved in memory. Again, they found that nerve stem cells transplanted into the brain survived, migrated to where they were needed and developed into specific cell types. Most significantly they resulted in improved memory. Russian scientists meanwhile, have shown that stem cells injected into the veins of rats suffering the effects of stroke helped reduce the stroke-related damage and preserve the cognitive functions of the animals.

These are just some of the many experiments going on around the world investigating the use of stem cells in the brain. Already, stem cells are used to treat humans – for example, to replace bone marrow in cancer patients. As our ability to use these cells grows, it seems likely that our brains are going to reap the benefits.

Conclusion

Hopefully, reading this book has left you with a sense that your own intellectual powers are something you have the power to enhance. Whoever you are, the choices you make every day have an impact on mental sharpness. Fingers crossed, you also have a better sense of what to do – and what to avoid – if you want to stay in peak intellectual condition as you grow older.

As we have seen, this book combines research in areas that some experts might consider distinct: intelligence, memory, attention, age-related cognitive decline and so on. In part, this has been a pragmatic decision: getting bogged down in exactly what 'intelligence' is might be important in an academic sense but it doesn't really help in our day-to-day dealings with our own intelligence. If you are adept at reading and responding to others' emotions, you are referred to as having a high 'emotional intelligence'; whether or not it can strictly be called 'intelligence', if this skill helps you get the most out of life, then surely it's important.

For most of us, 'intelligence' is simply the combination of mental skills that help us get along in the world. If getting a good night's sleep helps you ace an important job interview, then it's worth doing, regardless of whether or not it influences the 'general intelligence' that an IQ test tries to measure.

The mixing together of disciplines in this book is also a reflection of the fact that the science of intelligence is still very much a developing field. Our understanding of how the brain works still has a long way to go; not to mention our understanding of what characteristics of the brain relate to the skills that intelligence tests measure. In the meantime, the best we can do is remember that our brains are part of our bodies. They rely on the oxygen carried by red blood cells and are influenced by our hormones. Most importantly, they respond well to rest, good diet and a judicious bit of exercise, both physical and mental.

And if researchers are only beginning to discover exactly what kinds of exercise are most effective at maintaining life-long brain health, that isn't an excuse to sit back and do nothing. Thanks to advances in public health and medicine, the average human life expectancy is extending. Keeping your wits about you for the long haul will become more and more important. So get out there; stretch yourself. Hopefully the information in this book will steer you in the right direction in making changes to your lifestyle. Try new things. It's the smart thing to do.

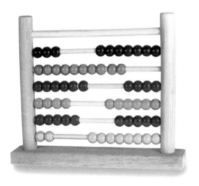

Resources

PART ONE:

1. Breastfeeding
http://jech.bmj.com/cgi/content/abstract/59/2/130
http://www.who.int/topics/breastfeeding/en/
Kramer, MS et al, Breastfeeding and child cognitive development, *Archives of General Psychiatry* 2008;65:578-584.

2. Childhood mistreatment
Slade EP & Wissow LS, The influence on childhood maltreatment on adolescents academic performance, *Economics and Education Review*, 2007;26:604-614.
Strathearn, L, Childhood neglect and cognitive development in extremely low birth weight infants: a prospective study, *Pediatrics* 2001;108:142-151.

3. Early crawling
http://www3.interscience.wiley.com/journal/118545435/abstract?CRETRY=1&SRETRY=0
Piek JP et al The role of early fine and gross motor development on later motor ad cognitive ability, *Human Movement Science*, 2008;27:668-681.
Campos JJ et al Travel broadens the mind, *Infancy*, 2000;2:149-219.

4. Maternal drug use
http://ohioline.osu.edu/hyg-Fact/5000/5535.html
http://babyfit.sparkpeople.com/articles.asp?id=783
http://www.ncsl.org/programs/health/forum/maternalabuse.htm

5. Having a younger father
Saha S, et al, Advanced paternal age is associated with impaired neuro-cognitive outcomes during infancy and childhood, *PLoS* Medicine 2009;6: e1000040.
http://medicine.plosjournals.org/archive/1549-1676/6/3/pdf/10.1371_journal.pmed.1000040-S.pdf

6. Infant nutrition
Ritter L et al Growth and intellectual development, *Pediatrics* 1986;78;646-650.
http://jn.nutrition.org/cgi/content/abstract/129/12/2196

7. Low birth weight
http://www.pubmedcentral.nih.gov/articlerender.fcgi?artid=37317
http://www.pubmedcentral.nih.gov/articlerender.fcgi?artid=1177

8. Being tall
Gale C, Commentary: Height and intelligence, *International Journal of Epidemiology* 2005;34:678-679.

9. High-quality pre-school
http://www.fpg.unc.edu/~abc/
http://highscope.org/Content.asp?ContentId=219
http://childtrends.org/lifecourse/programs/CarolinaAbecedarian-Program.htm

10. High testosterone levels
http://www.autismresearchcentre.com/arc
http://www.monash.edu.au/news/mar08-dementia.html
http://www3.interscience.wiley.com/journal/118692229/abstract
http://www.nia.nih.gov/NewsAndEvents/PressReleases/PR200 21104Free.htm

11. Higher socio-economic class
Nettle, D, Intelligence and class mobility in the British population, *British Journal of Psychology* (2003), 94, 551 – 561
http://www.time.com/time/time100/scientist/other/iq.html

12. Poverty
Brooks-Gunn J & Duncan GJ The effects of poverty on children, *The Future of Children* 1997;7:55-71.
http://michna.com/intelligence.htm

13. HIV
http://www.who.int/features/qa/71/en/index.html

14. Kidney disease
http://esciencenews.com/articles/2008/11/06/kidney.transplantation.provides.cognitive.benefits.patients.with.kidney.disease
Hailpern SM, et al Moderate chronic kidney disease and cognitive function in adults 20 to 59 years of age: third national health an nutrition examination survey, *Journal of the American Society of Nephrology* 2007;18:2205-2213.

15. Chemotherapy
http://www.cancer.org/docroot/MBC/content/MBC_2_3x_Che mobrain.asp
http://www.sciencedaily.com/releases/2006/10/061006072544.ht

16. Thyroid disease
Tan ZS, et al, Thyroid function and the risk of Alzheimer disease, *Archives of Internal Medicine* 2008;168:1514-1520.
Volpato S, et al Serum thyroxine level and cognitive decline in euthyroid older women, *Neurology* 2002;58:1055-1061.

17. Mental health problems

http://med.stanford.edu/news_releases/2005/november/bipo-lar.html

http://en.wikipedia.org/wiki/List_of_people_believed_to_have_b een_affected_by_bipolar_disorder

Jamison KR. Touched with fire: manic-depressive illness and the artistic temperament. *Free Press* 1993

18. Ageing

http://www.nlm.nih.gov/medlineplus/dementia.html

McClearn, G, et al, Substantial Genetic Influence on Cognitive Abilities in Twins 80 or More Years Old, *Science*, 1997; 226:1560-1563.

19. Living in modern times

Flynn J What is intelligence, *Cambridge University Press*, 2007.

http://www.indiana.edu/~intell/flynneffect.shtml

20. Genetic inheritance

http://www.eurekalert.org/pub_releases/2009-02/aaon-hap021009.php

PART TWO:

21. A good night's sleep

Drummond SPA et al Altered brain response to verbal learning following sleep deprivation, Nature 2000;403:655-657.

Luber B et al Remediation of Sleep-Deprivation—Induced Working Memory Impairment with fMRI-Guided Transcranial Magnetic Stim-ulation Cerebral Cortex, *Cerebral Cortex* 2008;18:2077-2085

Ellebogen JM Cognitive benefits of sleep and their loss due to sleep deprivation, *Neurology* 2005;64:E25-E27.

http://health.ucsd.edu/news/2000_02_09_Sleep.html

22. Sleep apnea

Beebe DW Neural and neurobehavioral dysfunction in children with obstructive sleep apnea, *PloS Medicine* 2006;3:1220-1221.

Alchanatis M, et al, Sleep apnea-related cognitive deficits and intelligence: an implication of cognitive reserve theory. *Journal of Sleep Research* 2005;14:69-75.

http://www.hopkinsmedicine.org/Press_re-leases/2006/08_21_06

23. Antidepressant medication

http://psy.psychiatryonline.org/cgi/content/full/43/1/31

Talan J, Common drugs may cause cognitive problems, *Neurology* ow 2008;4:10-11.

24. View of trees

http://www.boston.com/bostonglobe/ideas/arti-cles/2009/01/04/how_the_city_hurts_your_brain/

http://www.sciencedaily.com/re-leases/2009/02/090217092758.htm

25. Sunshine

http://www.sciencentral.com/articles/view.php3?article_id=218 392467&cat=1_7

http://www.sciencedaily.com/re-leases/2009/01/090122093918.htm

Vandewalle G, et al, Daytime light exposure dynamically en-hances brain responses, *Current Biology* 2006;16:1616-1621.

26. Pregnancy

http://www.theaustralian.news.com.au/story/0,25197,2447828 9-23289,00.html

http://www.guardian.co.uk/science/2009/feb/08/pregnancy-maternity-sharpen-womens-brains

27. Stress

http://www.find-health-articles.com/rec_pub_17572832-cogni-tive-function-outpatients-perceived-chronic-stress.htm

Saltzman KM, et al, IQ and post-traumatic stress symptoms in children exposed to interpersonal violence, 2006;36:261.

http://www.sciencedaily.com/re-leases/2008/03/080314085041.htm

28. Being sociable

http://www.timesonline.co.uk/tol/life_and_style/article640746.ec e?token=null&offset=0&page=1

http://www.nytimes.com/2008/05/13/health/13brain.html

http://www.pnas.org/content/99/7/4436.abstract

29. Depression

Delaloye C, et al, Cognitive impairment in late-onset depression, European Neurology 2008;60:149-154.

Austin M-P, et al, Cognitive deficits in depression, *The British Journal of Psychiatry* 2001;178:200-206.

http://bjp.rcpsych.org/cgi/content/abstract/163/3/338

30. Getting an education

Ceci S, How much does schooling influence general intelligence and its cognitive components? *Developmental Psychology* 1991;27:703-722.

31. Cohabiting

http://well.blogs.nytimes.com/2008/08/01/marriage-divorce-and-alzheimers-risk/

http://www.medpagetoday.com/MeetingCoverage/ICAD/10334

32. Loneliness

Ertel KA, et al, Effects of Social Integration on Preserving Memory Function in a Nationally Representative US Elderly Population, *American Journal of Public Health 2008*;98:1215-1220.

Heinrich L and Gullone E, The clinical significance of loneliness: A literature review, Clinical Psychology Review 2006;26:695-718.

33. Leaving work early

Virtanen M, et al, Long working hours and cognitive function, *American Journal of Epidemiology* 2009.

34. Napping

Hayashi M, et al, The effects of a 20 min nap in the mid-afternoon on mood, performance and EEG activity, *Clinical Neurophysiology* 1999; 110:272-279.

Tietzel, AJ, Lack LC, The short-term benefits of brief and long naps following nocturnal sleep restriction, *Sleep.* 2001; 24:293-300.

35. Diabetes

Gregg EW, et al Is diabetes associated with cognitive impairment and cognitive decline among older women? *Archives of Internal Medicine* 2000;160:174-180.

Saczynski JS, et al, Cognitive Impairments: an increasingly important complication of type 2 diabetes, *American Journal of Epidemiology* 2008; 168:1132-1139.

36. Silica in water

Rondeau V, et al Aluminium and Silica in Drinking Water and Risk of Alzheimer s Disease or Cognitive Decline: Findings from 15-year Follow-up of PAQUID Cohort, *American Journal of Epidemiology* 2008;doi: 10.1093/aje/kwn348.

http://www.waterquality.crc.org.au/hsarch/HS46n.htm

37. Heavy metal poisoning

http://emedicine.medscape.com/article/814960-overview

http://www.answers.com/topic/heavy-metal-poisoning

Torrente M, et al Metal concentrations in hair and cognitive assessment in an adolescent population, *Biological Trace Element Research* 2005;104:215-221.

38. Iron deficiency

http://www.eurekalert.org/pub_releases/2004-04/foas-mid040404.php

http://www.pop.psu.edu/searchable/press/apr2104.htm

Lozoff B, Jimenez E, and Wolf AW, Long-term developmental outcome of infants with iron deficiency, *New England Journal of Medicine* 1991; 325:687-694.

39. Creatine

McMorris T, et al Creatine supplementation and cognitive performance in elderly individuals, *Neuropsychology, Development and Cognition Section B: Aging, Neuropsychology and Cognition*, 2007;14:517-528.

McMorrisT, et al Effect of creatine supplementation and sleep deprivation, with mild exercise, on cognitive and psychomotor performance, mood state and plasma concentration of catecholamines and cortisol, *Psychopharmacology* 2006;185:93-103.

40. Vitamin B12

Smith AD & Refsum H Vitamin B-12 and cognition in the elderly, *American Journal of Clinical Nutrition* 2009;89:707S-711S.

Vogiatzoglou A, et al Vitamin B12 status and rate of brain volume loss in community-dwelling elderly, *Neurology* 2008;71:826-832.

41. Ginkgo biloba

Le Bars PL, et al A placebo-controlled, double-blind, randomized trial of an extract of Ginkgo biloba for dementia. North American Egb study group, *Journal of the American Medical Association* 1997;278:1327-1332.

DeKosky ST, et al Ginkgo biloba for prevention of dementia, *Journal of the American Medical Association* 2008;300:2253-2262.

http://general-medicine.jwatch.org/cgi/content/full/2008/1126/1

42. Eating regular meals

Benton D & Parker P Breakfast, blood glucose and cognition, *American Journal of Clinical Nutrition* 1998;67 Suppl: 772S.

Knarek R. Psychological effects of snacks and altered meal frequency, *British Journal of Nutrition* 1997;77 Suppl 1:S105-S120.

Smith A, et al Effects of evening meal and caffeine on cognitive performance, mood and cardiovascular functioning the following day, *Journal of Psychopharmacology* 1993;7:203-206

43. Eating fish

Morris MC, et al Fish consumption and cognitive decline with age in a large community study, *Archives of Neurology* 2005;62:184901853.

http://www.dha-in-mind.com/omega-3+dha+in+the+news.aspx?newsid372=6&&Fish-Slows-Cognitive-Decline-Increases-Infants-Cognitive-Ability&

Fontani G, et al Cognitive and physiological effects of Omega-3 polyunsaturated fatty acid supplementation in healthy subjects, *European Journal of Clinical Investigation* 2005;35:691-699.

http://www.americanheart.org/presenter.jhtml?identifier=3013797

44. Early onset of obesity

Miller J, et al, Neurocognitive findings in Prader-Willi syndrome and early onset morbid obesity, *Journal of Pediatrics* 2006;149:192-198.

http://www.who.int/dietphysicalactivity/publications/facts/obesity/en/

45. Eating animal fats
http://neurology.org/cgi/content/abstract/62/2/275
http://www.handcoding.com/archives/2004/10/28/trans-fat-could-impair-memory-and-intellect/

46. Blueberries
http://www.apa.org/monitor/dec01/blueberries.html
Casadesus G et al Modulation of hippocampal plasticity and cognitive behaviour by short-term blueberry supplementation aged rats *Nutritional Neuroscience* 2004;7:309-316.

47. High blood pressure
http://aje.oxfordjournals.org/cgi/content/abstract/138/6/353
http://jama.ama-assn.org/cgi/content/abstract/274/23/1846

48. Eating tofu
Grodstein R, Stampfer MJ Tofu and Cognitive Function: Food for Thought, *Journal of the American College of Nutrition* 2000;19:207-209.
Hogervorst E, et al High Tofu Intake is Associated with Worse Memory in Elderly Indonesian Men and Women, *Dementia and Geriatric Cognitive Disorders* 2008;26:50-57.

49. Eating your greens
Morris MC, et al Associations of vegetable and fruit consumption with age-related cognitive change, *Neurology* 2006;67:1370-1376.

50. Smoking
Whalley LJ, et al Childhood IQ, smoking and cognitive change from age 11 to 64 years, *Addictive Behaviours* 2005;30:77-88.
Glass JM, et al Smoking is associated with neurocognitive deficits in alcoholism, *Drug and Alcohol Dependence* 2006;82:119-126.
http://www.who.int/tobacco/en/

51. Drinking coffee
Smith AP, et al Investigation of the effects of coffee on alertness and performance during the day and night, *Neuropsychobiology* 1993;27:217-223.
http://www.thetechherald.com/article.php/200844/2350/Study-finds-scientific-basis-for-coffee-s-stimulating-effect
http://www.nationmaster.com/graph/foo_cof_con-food-coffee-consumption

52. Marijuana
Goldschmidt L, et al Prenatal marijuana exposure and intelligence test performance at age 6, *Journal of the American Academy of Child & Adolescent Psychiatry*, 2008;47:254-263.

http://www.newscientist.com/article/dn2140-marijuana-does-not-dent-iq-permanently.html

53. Ecstasy
http://www.admin.cam.ac.uk/news/press/dpp/2002061801
Schilt T, et al Cognition in Novice Estasy Users with Minimal Exposure to Other Drugs, *Archives of General Psychiatry* 2007;64:728-736.

54. Alcoholism
http://pubs.niaaa.nih.gov/publications/aa53.htm
http://pubs.niaaa.nih.gov/publications/aa04.htm

55. Alcohol in moderation
http://news.bbc.co.uk/2/hi/health/1058526.stm
http://content.nejm.org/cgi/content/abstract/352/3/245

PART THREE:
56. Brain training
http://www.sciencedaily.com/releases/2008/06/080605163804.htm
Jaeggi SM et al, Improving fluid intelligence with training on working memory, *PNAS* 2008.

57. Head Start programme
http://www.acf.hhs.gov/programs/ohs/
http://www.acf.hhs.gov/programs/opre/hs/impact_study/index.html

58. Brain games
http://technology.timesonline.co.uk/tol/news/tech_and_web/gadgets_and_gaming/article5587314.ece
http://www.ltscotland.org.uk/ictineducation/gamesbasedlearning/sharingpractice/braintraining/introduction.asp

59. Mnemonics
http://www.eudesign.com/mnems/_mnframe.htm

60. Critical thinking
http://highered.mcgraw-hill.com/sites/0767417399/student_view0/chapter1/chapter_outline.html
Halpern, DF Teaching critical thinking for transfer across domains, *American Psychologist* 1998;53:449-455.

61. Playing computer games
http://www.webmd.com/parenting/guide/video-games-tv-do-they-make-kids-smarter?page=2
http://abcnews.go.com/wnt/health/story?id=814080

62. Listening to music
http://www.nyas.org/annals/annalsExtra.asp?annalID=10
http://news.bio-medicine.org/biology-news-3/Music-thought-

to-enhance-intelligence mental-health-and-immune-system-6208-1/

63. Playing an instrument
Foregard M, et al Practicing a musical instrument in childhood is associated with enhanced verbal ability and nonverbal reasoning, *PloS One* 2008
Vaughn K Music and mathematics: Modest support for the oft-claimed relationship. *J Aesthet Educ* 2000;34:149—166.

64. Early exposure to TV
Zimmerman FJ, et al, "Children's television viewing and cognitive outcomes," *Archives of Pediatrics and Adolescent Medicine* 2005;159:619-625.

65. Playing chess
http://www.uschessmates.com/1indexpage/article1.html
Liptrap JM, et al Chess and standard test scores, *Chess Life* 1998; March:41-43.

66. Learning a new skill
http://www.ucl.ac.uk/news/news-articles/08010/08101706
http://www.amaassn.org/amednews/2008/11/17/hlsa1117.htm

67. Becoming a taxi driver
http://news.bbc.co.uk/1/hi/sci/tech/677048.stm
Maguire EA, et al Navigation-related structural change in the hippocampi of taxi drivers, *PNAS* 2000;97:4398-4403.

68. Learning another language
Foster KM & Reeves CK Foreign language in the elementary school improves cognitive skills *FLES News* 1989;2:4.
Samuels DD & Griffore RJ The Plattsburgh French language immersion programL its influence on intelligence and self esteem *Language Learning* 1979;29:45-52.

69. Being creative
Sternberg RJ, Kaufman JC and Grigorenko EL, *Applied Intelligence*, Cambridge University Press, 2008.
http://www.kidsource.com/kidsource/content4/creativity.eq.html

70. Crafts
http://news.bbc.co.uk/2/hi/health/7896441.stm

71. Gardening
Simons LA, et al Lifestyle factors and risk of dementia: Dubbo Study of the elderly, *Medical Journal of Australia* 2006;184:68-70.

72. Learning philosophy as a child
http://news.bbc.co.uk/1/hi/scotland/6330631.stm

73. Reading a book
Castro-Caldas A, et al The illiterate brain, *Brain* 1998; 121:1053-1063.
Stanovich KE Does reading make you smarter? *Advances in Child Development and Behaviour* 1993;24:133-180.

74. Meditation
http://www.sciencedaily.com/releases/2007/06/070625193240.htm
Valentine ER & Sweet PLG Meditation and attention: a comparison of the effects of concentrative and mindfulness meditation on sustained attention, *Mental Health, Religion and Culture* 1999;2:59-70.
Topping KJ & Trickey S Collaborative philosophical enquiry for school children: Cognitive effects at 10-12 years, *Educational Psychology* 2007;77:271-288.

75. Physical exercise
http://www.sciencedaily.com/releases/2004/10/041019082604.htm

76. Dancing
http://www.ama-assn.org/amednews/2008/11/17/hlsa1117.htm
http://aip.org/dbis/stories/2004/14037.html

77. Yoga
Chattha R, et al, Effect of yoga on cognitive functions in climacteric syndrome: a randomized control study, *British Journal of Obstetrics and Gynaecology* 2008;115:991-1000.
http://seniorjournal.com/NEWS/Alzheimers/2007/7-06-12-DailyYoga.htm

78. Tai chi
http://news.illinois.edu/news/08/1205dementia.html
http://www.pdf.org/en/pubs_scientists/e_quality/18487897

79. Boxing
Mendez MF, The neuropsychiatric aspects of boxing, *International Journal of Psychiatry in Medicine*, 1995;25:249-262.
Roberts GW, et al The occult afternrath of boxing, *Journal of Neurology, Neurosurgery and Psychiatry* 1990;53:373-378.

80. Taking a walk
http://www.thetakeaway.org/stories/2008/nov/13/cognitive-benefits-interacting-nature-walking-makes-your-smart/
http://www.spring.org.uk/2009/01/memory-improved-20-by-nature-walk.php

PART FOUR:
81. Grey matter
http://www.bioedonline.org/news/news.cfm?art=1170
http://www.futurepundit.com/archives/002244.html

82. White matter
http://today.uci.edu/news/release_detail.asp?key=1261

83. Small brain
http://www.news.vcu.edu/news.aspx?v=detail&nid=1268
http://www.gvsu.edu/psychology/index.cfm?id=5FA88B73-
D3D6-5B74-66B17C5AB4640467

84. Fast brainwaves
http://www.nature.com/neuro/journal/v6/n3/abs/nn1014.html
Gray JR, et al, Neural mechanisms of general fluid intelligence,
Nature Neuroscience 2003;6:316-322.
Mariboru U, et al, Differences in event-related and induced
brain oscillations in the theta and alpha frequency bands related
to human intelligence, Neuroscience Letters 2000;293:191-194.

85. Energy-hungry brain
http://www.psych.utoronto.ca/users/reingold/courses/intelli-
gence/cache/1198gottfred.html
http://www.thefreelibrary.com/Brain+clues+to+energy-
efficient+learning-a012123949

86. Brain injury
http://braininjury.org.au/portal/
http://www.headinjury.com/

87. Stroke
http://www.strokefoundation.com.au/preventing-a-stroke
Tatemichi TK, et al, Cognitive impairment after stroke: frequency, patters and relationship to functional abilities, Journal
of Neurology, Neurosurgery and Psychiatry 1994;57:202-207.
Del Ser T Evolution of cognitive impairment after stroke and risk
factors for delayed progression Stroke 2005;36:2670.

88. Fast nerves
Petrill SA, et al The independent prediction of general intelligence by elementary cognitive tasks: Genetic and environmental influences, Behavior Genetics 1996;24:135-147.

89. Thin cerebral cortex
http://www.washingtonpost.com/wp-dyn/content/article/
2006/03/29/AR2006032902182.html
Shaw P, et al, Intellectual ability and cortical development
in children and adolescents, Nature 2006;440:676-679.
http://www.sciencemag.org/cgi/content/sum-
mary/311/5769/1851

90. Epilepsy
http://www.epilepsy.com/articles/ar_1064856376
Helmstaedter C, et al Chronic epilepsy and cognition: a
longitudinal study in temporal lobe epilepsy, Annals of
Neurology 2003;54:425-432

91. Phenylketonuria
http://en.wikipedia.org/wiki/Phenylketonuria#Pathophysiology
Channon S, et al, Effects of dietary management of phenylketonuria on long-term cognitive outcome, Archives of Disease
in Childhood 2007;92:213-218.

92. Magnetic stimulation
http://www.news-medical.net/?id=34916
http://www.infrapsych.com/content/general/TMS.html

93. Neurodegeneration
Cunningham C, et al Systemic inflammation induces acute
behavioural and cognitive changes and accelerates
neurodegenerative disease, Biological Psychiatry 2009;
65:304-312.
http://www.huliq.com/11/75894/common-mechanism-may-
underlie-many-neurodegenerative-diseases

94. Concussion
http://www.eurekalert.org/pub_releases/2009-01/oup-
cif012609.php
http://www.medpagetoday.com/CriticalCare/HeadTrauma/12623

95. Nanobots
http://en.wikipedia.org/wiki/Ray_Kurzweil
http://news.bbc.co.uk/2/hi/americas/7248875.stm

96. Artificial intelligence
http://singinst.org/

97. Supplemental brains
http://www.eecg.toronto.edu/~mann/
http://query.nytimes.com/gst/fullpage.html?res=940CE0D7123
9F937A25750C0A9649C8B63

98. Brain drugs
http://findarticles.com/p/articles/mi_m1568/is_9_34/ai_966448
74)
http://www.wired.com/medtech/drugs/news/2008/04/smart_
drugs

99. Genetic engineering
http://www.drugresearcher.com/Emerging-targets/Increased-
intelligence-through-genetic-engineering
http://www.aboutintelligence.co.uk/genetic-engineering-boost-
intelligence.html

100. Stem cells
Brannen Qu T et al Human neural stem cells improve cognitive
function of aged brain, Neuroreport. 2001;12:1127-1132.
Yamasaki TR et al Neural stem cells improve memory in an
inducible mouse model of neuronal loss, Journal of
Neuroscience 2007;27:11925-11933.

Index